A SHELTER FROM THE STORM

A SHELTER FROM THE STORM

an ordinary childhood
in an extraordinary time 1935–45

by David Jupp

Spinnaker
Press

Portsmouth

A SHELTER FROM THE STORM

First published in 2012
By Spinnaker Press Ltd

ISBN: 978-0-95666 19-3-7
Copyright © David Jupp, 2012

Cover design and artwork by David Jupp

Printed and bound in the UK
by Biddles, King's Lynn

To the memory
of

my parents and sister

Hannah Sophia
born 15 December 1893
died 7 December 1967

Albert Ernest
born 6 July 1891
died 10 December 1976

Irene Annie
born 9 March 1921
died 6 December 1995

Acknowledgements

My thanks to my wife Suzanne
for all her help and valuable suggestions
that have enriched this book

To my brother Albert (Bert)
for his encouragement and support not only during
this project but throughout my life

also I would like to thank my four children
Stephen, Christopher, Jon, Emma
for all their interest, suggestions and help
with special thanks to Emma who initiated this book
and helped in so many ways
and in particular Stephen for his enthusiasm,
and hard work in making this publication possible

Finally my thanks to all at *'Spinnaker Press'*
especially to Dale Gunthorp for her initial encouragement
and belief in this book and for her further suggestions
and editorial direction

David Jupp

The Author and Publisher
would like to express their thanks
for the kind permissions to use the
following material

The map shown on the front cover
from the Reader's Digest Great World Atlas (1968)
with permission from the International Managing Editor
Reader's Digest Books and Home Entertainment
Pegasus Regional Limited

The locomotive shown on the back cover
with permission from the Administrative Manager
Didcot Railway Centre
Berkshire

The lyrics from 'Roll Out the Barrel'
(Beer Barrel Polka)
with permission from
prof@diamondgeezers.org.uk

Contents

Author's Note

An ordinary childhood in an extraordinary time

THERE CAN BE LITTLE DOUBT THAT THE 'Thirties' and 'Forties' were extraordinary. It is, however, less certain that any childhood should be called ordinary for each child is unique.

Children live in two worlds, their own and the larger world outside. Writing as a 'grown-up' but from the viewpoint of a child I have endeavoured to bring these two worlds together and through each episode to capture fragments of a childhood long ago.

I am quite sure there are inaccuracies and some of the events described may not be strictly chronological. At times I have used my imagination and added a little colouring but, for the most part, the people and events described are just as I remember them.

A Shelter from the Storm

Isaiah 25 v 4

A Shelter as portrayed in this book can have three different interpretations. The physical construction: the corrugated air raid shelter in the garden and the safe place beneath the stairs.

The psychological Shelter that the family were able to create around David's young life, by maintaining a sense of calm and normality in the face of both employment uncertainty and in the midst of war.

And finally the Shelter of a child's world where imagination, adventure and the serious business of play all take precedence over the concerns of the adult world.

Stephen Jupp

Prologue

Rain, rain, go away . . .

STORM CLOUDS *hung low over the Reigate hills and rain swept across the little town nestled in the Holmesdale Valley below. Traffic, with wipers whirring, slowed through the High Street, and on the pavements pedestrians, bent beneath umbrellas, hurried about their business not stopping to pass the time of day.*

Reigate's Priory Park, the heathland and commons were deserted while up and down the side roads, except for the tradesmen, the baker, milkman and postman, there was little sign of life.

In Doods Road, not far from Wray Common with its picturesque windmill, a small child with his face pressed hard against the attic bedroom window, drew patterns with his finger and watched the rain slanting against the glass panes, splashing on to the window ledge, almost obscuring the garden below.

'When will it stop?' I asked.

My Mother, who was busying herself in the bedroom, came over and stood beside me and we both looked out at the rain.

'When will it go away?' I asked again.

1

Mother, who was never very far away, smiled and placed her arm around my shoulder.

'When I was a little girl,' she said, 'we used to say this rhyme:'

Rain, rain, go away; Come again another day!'

'And did it go away?' I questioned.

'Sometimes, it did.' She said.

And so I repeated it after her and then said it over and over again:

Rain, rain, go away; Come again another day!'

And, of course, the rain did stop, although I can't be sure it stopped on that day. The angry clouds did disperse, the sun shone once more, but unbeknown to me (I was only three years old) other clouds were forming, darker and so much more threatening. They were destined to remain for a long time and it would take more than a simple rhyme to despatch them.

The year was nineteen thirty-nine and Mr Churchill, echoed by others, spoke of *"The Gathering Storm."* Already storm clouds were fast gathering over Europe and were heading towards us.

War was a word I was yet to hear, certainly not to understand, yet war was on the horizon and it would bring change to all our lives.

Beginnings

An Introduction

ON A THURSDAY, the twelfth of September nineteen thirty-five, Hannah Sophia Jupp gave birth to a baby boy.

When my mother had first discovered she was again pregnant it had come as a great shock not only to her but also to my father. Mother was now into her forties; possibly starting the 'change' and thinking her child-bearing days were over, until a visit to the doctor proved otherwise and an examination confirmed I was on my way!

To make matters worse this was the depressed thirties, a time of change and uncertainty. My Father, Albert Ernest (everyone knew him as Ern), was a carpenter and joiner, not the most secure of trades in those days; often he would be in and out of work and was about to be laid off in the immediate future. But if this unplanned pregnancy was a shock to my parents, my arrival into the world was an even greater shock to my brother.

Bert had just turned thirteen. He had completely failed to notice anything odd in mother's changing shape and the first he knew of my impending birth was as he lay in bed and heard cries from the downstairs bedroom. It was at this time that Dad took the opportunity to share with him some of the facts of life! Later that same morning, before going to school, Bert peeped into his parent's bedroom and glimpsed his newly born brother in Mother's arms.

His sister, Renie, who was sixteen months older must have surely known what was about to take place but, if she had, she kept it to herself. As the only daughter it would now fall on her to play an important part in helping Mother with my early upbringing and sharing in some of the extra work this would entail.

As soon as my parents were able, I was taken to our local church for a service of dedication. Recently the family had started attending the Elim Foursquare Gospel Church. This was quite a departure for my Dad who like his father had been a staunch Anglican, but that had changed and the less formal service now appealed to both Mother and Father and to the other members of the family.

In the presence of that little congregation, in a simple act of dedication, my parents handed me to the

Pastor, I was prayed over, presented before the Lord, and named.

'What do you name this child?' asks the Pastor.

'We name him *David*.'

I was now handed back to my parents who would proudly show off their new arrival and latest addition to the *Jupp* family.

One

Moving

AFTER WEEKS OF agonizing indecision and discussion it was finally agreed we would be moving from Reigate to Portsmouth. Not that I had any say in it; I was now only four years old, but our regular milkman had plenty to say and what he said was not exactly a source of encouragement.

'*Portsmouth? Did you say Portsmouth?* You're not going to Portsmouth!' and shaking his head added, 'That's a dump, that is; a proper dump!'

I had no idea what a dump might be, especially a proper dump, but it certainly sounded interesting. Apparently our milkman's knowledge of Portsmouth had been acquired whilst serving in the Royal Navy. However all his well-intentioned warnings were in vain. The decision to leave Reigate had been made and was final, there was no going back.

The date for our move was set and, early one sunny morning in May, aproned removal men arrived and promptly set to work, carrying furniture and other items, piece by piece, until all had been loaded into the large removal van, and with each room stripped of its contents, leaving the house empty, hollow and forlorn.

It had been agreed that Dad would ride in the van and accompany the men to Portsmouth while Mother, my brother Bert and I would follow by train later. My sister Renie was at this time working in London and had found accommodation there.

Before we could leave Mother had insisted on a final tidy up.

'You have to leave it as you'd expect to find it,' she said in her soft Suffolk voice and getting down on her knees she set to work scrubbing the linoleum floors until she was satisfied that all was, as she put it, *'shipshape and in order!'*

Meanwhile, I found myself standing alone in the corner of our now bare living room. Suddenly I was puzzled, upset and almost on the verge of panic. It was not that I didn't want to leave my Doods Road house, it was just that I had made a fearful discovery, my voice no longer belonged to me. I didn't sound like me any more! I began to shout, louder and louder. It brought my big brother running over to me. I was now in tears.

'Whatever is the matter, David?'

I tried, as best I could, to make him understand.

Fortunately he seemed to grasp my dilemma and took the time to explain in simple terms about acoustics and echoes and empty rooms.

'Listen,' he said. 'My voice sounds different too!'

And he shouted to prove it. I was immediately reassured, we both laughed and at this point Mother returned.

'Well, I think we're almost done now,' she said and added, 'Just a little more to do and we'll be off.'

And so we prepared to say our final goodbyes.

I took a parting glance at my garden. It had always been such a special place for me, filled with many wonderful and happy childhood memories that would remain with me for ever. I had played there and day-dreamed, living in an imaginary world of my own, safe, sheltered and cocooned from the real world outside.

From the window I could see my very own part of the garden, a small plot that my brother had staked out for me and where I could dig to my hearts content.

Once my big sister, Renie, had come to see what I was up to. She looked very smart in her flower patterned dress making her look slim and grown-up, (she was after all nearly eighteen years old). She moved closer and seemed very impressed with my digging.

'What an enormous big hole,' she said. 'If you dig any deeper you'll reach Australia!'

After further explanation that Australia lay beneath

us and on the other side of the world I summoned up new energy and determination and continued digging until tea-time. The hole got deeper and deeper. I even put my ear to the ground thinking I might hear voices. There was only silence. I never did reach Australia!

Although I was excited at the thought of going to a new house in a big city, I also knew there would be much I would miss; much I would be leaving behind.

I was about to abandon my ageing tin car. It had given me so much pleasure but was now on its last legs, *or wheels*, and I had all but out-grown it. Sadly it had been decided to leave it behind.

My *crocodile pond* would also be staying. I called it that, though in fact it was only an old tin bath standing on a rickety table and leaking water through its rusting seams, but concealed beneath those murky depths was a crocodile!

Of course, the crocodile wasn't real, only made of lead; its coating of green paint had long disappeared but at some time, and I couldn't be sure when, I had placed it into the discoloured rain water where it had suddenly and mysteriously come to life and now appeared frighteningly real! When I was particularly brave I would stand on tiptoe and try to see my crocodile's scaly outline.

My brother, who was much older and wiser than me, would laugh good-naturally and tell me not to be so silly.

'Of course it isn't alive.' And just to prove it he plunged his own hand into the water bringing it out seconds later with two of his fingers missing! Then seeing my consternation, quickly revealed the other two fingers quite intact. But even this show of bravery had done little to convince me.

Suddenly Mother's voice broke through my reverie!

'Nearly time to go,' she called. 'Whatever we do we mustn't miss that train!'

But it was the trains I would miss most of all. Our very close vicinity to the noisy steam trains was, for my Mother, a cause for vexation, especially on a washday, but for me it was heaven. The sights, sounds and smells of those great engines as they steamed past our back garden were sheer intoxication.

At the very first puff of smoke, or at the sound of a throaty whistle, I would peddle my little car, or run as fast as I could until I reached the high iron railings at the end of the garden which separated us from the railway lines. Standing on tiptoe, and raising myself to my full height, I would wave to the passing train drivers and their passengers and sometimes they would smile at this little fair-haired boy and wave back.

In a very short while I too would be travelling on one of these trains. I would be the passenger; it would be my turn to wave.

'Are you ready!' Once again Mother called. Now it

really was time for us to leave. Last little bits and pieces were bundled together and Mother, firmly and finally, closed the front door.

Two

The Journey begins

THE GUARD PLACED THE WHISTLE to his lips, waved his green flag and slowly, almost as though it were in no great hurry to leave, the train steamed out of the little Reigate station. The journey to Portsmouth had begun.

We had managed to find an empty third class compartment and from where I was sitting I was able to catch the view from both windows. Gradually the train gathered speed until the houses and gardens that backed the railway track appeared to race past our carriage windows, only to disappear behind a cloud of white steam. The tall wooden telegraph poles flashed by as we sped through the open Surrey countryside and the little town where I had spent the first four years of my life was soon to become a memory.

I now moved to a seat in the corner of the carriage

sitting opposite my Mother and brother who were both engaged in quiet conversation. Bert, with his good looks, was as dark as I was fair, he was already my hero and because of our age difference was, in some ways, a second father to me. Mother was now in her forty-seventh year, and both Bert and my sister Renie would have grown up remembering her as she was when younger.

Her dark chestnut brown hair would have been perhaps longer then and her face less lined, but even now her eyes were bright and she still had that wonderful smile that could light up a room and win many a friendship. It certainly won my Dad. Her smile and laughter had captivated him. 'I was real taken by it,' he would say.

Mother was smiling now. 'Come and sit next to me,' she coaxed. I moved over and snuggled up beside her. These last years had been anxious times for all the family and traces of anxiety on Mother's face still remained.

Had I been a little older, perhaps I may have questioned why we were leaving the quietness and safety of Reigate to go to a city and seaport, whose shipping, dockyard and factories would doubtlessly soon become a strategic target for German bombers.

Although not fully able to understand what was happening I certainly was able to remember some of the events leading up to our present journey. Looking back it had really begun that day when my Dad was made redundant . . .

Redundancy

My Father had come home a little earlier than usual and had placed his carpenter's bag bulging with tools on the living room floor. I was somewhat in awe of him; his slender frame belied his height making him look taller than he really was. He stood in front of us, his cloth cap perched on his head and the carpenter's pencil still lodged behind one ear. He had a bombshell to deliver.

Mother spoke first. 'You're early, dear,' she said, 'is everything alright?' but she knew what he was about to say, even before he spoke.

'It's bad news, Mother.'

Her lips trembled. 'You've been laid off.'

He nodded. 'Laid off . . . Sacked! Got the sack!'

I struggled to understand what it could all mean. In my mind I imagined dad being tied up in an enormous brown sack which sounded very exciting and I decided I wanted a *'sack'* all of my own!

Mother was close to tears. 'Whatever will we do? What's to become of us?'

Dad placed his arm on her shoulder, almost brusquely, for he had never been a man to show his true emotions.

'Now don't you fret dear,' he said. 'Somehow we'll manage.' And then, hoping to reassure her, he continued. 'You wait and see. It'll all turn out alright'

This, of course, had not been the first time they had faced this situation and it certainly wouldn't be the last . . .

Meanwhile in the world outside my own, other events had been taking place that would not only affect our lives but the lives of millions.

A king had abdicated, another been crowned. In Germany an unlikely Austrian with a 'Charlie Chaplain' moustache was about to plunge the world into war, while a euphoric Prime Minister, optimistically holding aloft a small piece of paper, had proclaimed: 'Peace in our time!' And at Chartwell, not so many miles away, an old man, painting pictures and puffing at his cigars, prophesied and waited impatiently for a destiny to be fulfilled.

We are at war . . .

The next event would also play a significant part in our parents' decision. Sunday morning, September third, nineteen thirty-nine, had begun like any other Sunday. Dad and Bert, dressed in their best suits, had earlier gone to church, but Mother and I had stayed at home. The time was just after eleven o'clock.

I had followed Mother up the narrow stairs to the landing and it was then that we heard our very first Air Raid siren. It started suddenly - a loud undulating wail; a strange unearthly sound but one that would soon become increasingly familiar though no less frightening.

Immediately Mother went into action making sure that all the windows at the top of the house were tightly closed. I heard her say something that sounded like *'Gas!'* and then, returning she bent down, put her hands on my shoulders, and made me promise that I would stay exactly where I was.

'Whatever you do,' she said, 'you must be a very good boy and not move from this spot 'till I come back.'

There was something in both her look and the tone of her voice that left me in no doubt that this was one time I must be obedient. I watched as she disappeared down the stairs and heard her close the front door behind her to join neighbours gathering in the street below.

I stood perfectly still, almost an impossibility, for what seemed a very long time just staring at the faded wallpaper in front of me. I was still standing there when Mother returned. I had expected some praise but all she said was: 'I do wish that your Daddy and Bertie were home.'

We didn't have long to wait, for just after the siren

had sounded once more – this time the *'All-clear'* – my father and brother burst in; their faces flushed; both a little breathless and talking much faster than usual.

'Thank goodness you're back,' cried Mother. 'I was getting so worried.'

Apparently the air raid warning had been a false alarm, but the church service had been interrupted and the congregation dismissed with the news of Mr Chamberlain's broadcast message to the nation . . . *"I have to tell you that we are now at war with Germany."*

From somewhere Bert produced an oddly shaped wooden box which he said was a 'wireless set.' (I had never seen one before), but clambering on to the living room table, he began stretching a wire from it and trailing it along the picture rail. (This was its aerial).

Once in position we all grouped around the little wireless, which suddenly came to life, emitting loud howls, screeches, crackles and whistles. Knobs were turned and, amazingly, muffled voices began to emerge from it.

I squeezed myself between the grown-ups and stretched up to my full height getting as near to the box as possible. I heard the words – *'War'*–*'Germany'* – *'Poland'* – *'Bombs,'* then more crackles and hisses. Everyone looked very serious and worried. I moved quietly away from the table and began to play.

Both these events were to play a part in our future, but it would be a letter that would finally force the decision.

The letter . . .

When Mother picked up the letter that morning she little realised its importance and how it would affect all our lives.

'It's from your brother, Fred.' she said handing the letter to dad. She had recognised the writing.

Dad had two brothers, my uncle Frank who lived in neighbouring Redhill and uncle Fred. There would have been three brothers, but William had sadly died of a fever at the young age of twenty-two while stationed at Basra during the First World War.

Fred was the youngest of the brothers. At an early age he had joined the Royal Flying Corps as a pilot and his love for aviation had never left him. He was now working at the *Airspeed Factory* and heading up the design team in the experimental department at Portsmouth. In his letter he was offering both Dad and my brother work positions in the factory.

My Father, himself, was no stranger to working on aircraft and had been employed in a reserve occupation during the First World War making wooden propellers[1]. After much deliberation, Dad had opened his writing desk, selected pen and paper and had written his reply . . .

---

[1] This was highly skilled and tedious work. Each propeller was made up with strips of mahogany laminated together, sanded and shaped until they were perfectly smoothed and balanced

We had now reached the halfway point of our journey.

'All Change for Portsmouth!'

Our train slowed, the brakes applied, and with a last gasp of steam stopped noisily at Guildford station.

The megaphone boomed for the second time, and as quickly as we could we gathered our few belongings and made our way down through the long subway just in time to board the connecting train arriving from London, Waterloo. This was a fast electric train. We managed to find seats and were only just settled when the train slid away from the platform, plunging mole-like into the dark chalk faced Guildford tunnel until at last emerging into the dazzling sunshine beyond.

Now we were flying past fields and farms, stretches of water, tree clad banks and buildings. Past little stations so swiftly it was impossible to catch their names and then stopping only at the larger ones. *Haslemere, Godalming, Petersfield,* and now *Havant.*

'It won't be long now,' Bert observed. 'We must be almost there.' Mother nodded.

As we approached the city the countryside gradually gave way to more built-up areas, factories and warehouses, goods yards and larger buildings. There was row upon row of constricted houses and the road running along-side the train track seemed busy with traffic.

We were now nearing our final destination. The train swayed its way alongside the station and came to a halt. We stepped on to the hard cold platform. Our journey to Portsmouth was over. We had arrived.

Three

Portsmouth

WE LEFT THE PLATFORM and stepped out into a different world. The pace had quickened, the buildings larger, the roads wider, even the air we breathed was somehow different. A gentle but fresh sea breeze filled our lungs. This was Portsmouth. We had left the little town of Reigate and were now part of this great bustling city.

Portsmouth . . . home of the Royal Navy; with its great Dockyard still cradling Nelson's famous *HMS Victory*, and its natural harbour afloat with war ships; the High Street in Old Portsmouth with its Cathedral; the famous Hard, and all the streets leading from it, still alive with history. Beyond this lay the city centre with its fine buildings, churches, cinemas, shops and houses but the largest and most impressive of these was the Guildhall.

This great, grey stone building with its magnificent domed clock tower, dominated the Portsmouth skyline. The two majestic lions that guarded the grand entrance looked down at the square below where a mix of people, both young and old who, like the traffic, were coming and going in every direction.

From her plinth Queen Victoria sternly surveyed the scene. Had it not been for the increased presence of service personnel and the banks of sandbags piled high, everything might have appeared almost normal. But the city was already preparing for an imminent enemy attack, and high over the roof-tops, silver-grey barrage balloons, like huge floating elephants, hung strategically in the sky above.

The same men, women and children now crossing under the shadow of the old Queen would shortly be destined to witness the devastation of their city. "A smitten city" with buildings reduced to rubble; burnt out shells scarring the city skyline; others partly or completely demolished would leave ugly craters to fill with stagnant water.

But all this was future and far from our thoughts as Mother, Bert and I stood at the bus-stop eagerly anticipating our new home and location. 'This looks like our bus!' Bert had already spotted it coming across the bridge.

'Number eighteen, I think that's the one!'

The bus that eventually drew up beside us was a

very different one from the green buses I had been used to at Reigate. It was dark red in colour with an upstairs and downstairs and sprouting from its grey rooftop were two spindly black arms[2] each attached to an overhead network of electrified wires that seemed to cover much of the city.

'It's a trolley-bus,' Bert quickly explained as we climbed aboard.

I was fascinated. I wanted my own toy one. And I also wanted my own barrage balloon! Luckily, *Woolworth's* were able to supply both, but that would be later.

The bus conductor pressed the bell and effortlessly, almost silently, we were on our way. I sat with my face to the window absorbing new sights with so many thoughts chasing through my head only to be interrupted by the conductor.

'Next stop Priory Crescent! Milton Park!'

This would be our stop.

'Here you are, *my luv*,' said the friendly conductor turning to my mother. 'This is where you get off.'

I think I once heard mother say that it had taken her quite a little while to get used to all these 'Pompey endearments,' *(and I'm not sure that she ever did!)* however,

---

[2] It was not uncommon, especially at a junction for these arms to become disengaged from their overhead wires. When this happened the conductor would pull out a long bamboo pole from the underneath of the bus and endeavor, amid sparks, to hook them back on to their supply.

she was grateful for the further directions given as he pointed us on our way.

It was one of those wonderfully sunny days that so often make up a childhood memory. The sky a vivid blue and cloudless; the little trees in the park heavy with May blossom and the flower beds vibrant with colour.

Mother was enchanted. 'How lovely,' she said. 'Why, it's really beautiful.'

We walked on through the park, crossing first one, then another busy road, until eventually we found ourselves in Warren Avenue. We were almost home.

Four

Warren Avenue

'THERE IT IS!' It was Bert who saw it first. Standing almost halfway up the road was our removal van. Only a few hours previously it had stood outside our old house in Doods Road.

As we reached the front door Dad was there to greet us. With his jacket off and his sleeves rolled up, although still wearing his waistcoat, he was busy directing and supervising the removal men who were still hard at work unloading our furniture. Of special concern was the placing of his precious piano which he now shepherded safely against a wall in the almost empty front room.

One of the first things my brother did was to reclaim his Raleigh cycle, from the van, and to ride away for a very quick exploration of our new neighbourhood.

Meanwhile, my Mother, when she saw the house promptly fell in love with it. It had upstairs and downstairs bay windows with a small tiled forecourt and a neatly clipped privet hedge enclosed by green painted iron railings and gate. (Sadly, as the war progressed, these railings would be needed to help the war effort. Our house, along with many others, would be stripped of its decorative Victorian ironwork; later to be turned into munitions.)

The front door, which now stood wide open, was wood-grained and inset with lead-lined stained glass panels. The polished brass letterbox,[3] door knocker and bell, gleamed in the sunlight.

'Well, what do you think of it?'

'Wonderful!' Mother replied and her face was beaming.

As we walked through the hallway the stairs were on our right, to the left of us was the front room, and behind it, the kitchen. Directly in front of us was the living room, this would be the heart of the house. The sunlight streamed through the flower patterned windows and glass panelled door that opened on to a conservatory that ran the whole width of the house. This would prove to be a real sun-trap. *(Mum would grow her tomato plants here and display her collection of cacti.*

---

[3] Later cleaning the brass would become my Saturday morning job for which I would be rewarded with the handsome sum of sixpence pocket money!

Dad would rig up a narrow improvised work-bench, and sometimes on a sunny Sunday afternoon would lie on it and, precariously balanced, would bask in the sunlight, often drifting asleep, miraculously, without falling!)

Best of all, the conservatory housed an indoor toilet. This was indeed a luxury! In our Doods Road house, the toilet, (lavatory, we called it) was an outside one, which meant a walk down the garden in all weathers.

I followed Mother upstairs to the bedrooms. Across the landing another surprise awaited us; it was our very own bathroom. Mother clapped her hands in delight. No more tin baths on a Saturday bath night! Instead a white enamelled tub, large enough to stretch out in, and to sail my boats! There was also a wash basin and a large impressive copper geyser that, when lit roared into life, supplying us with hot, steaming, running water.

'What a lot I shall have to tell Renie!' Mother was already composing a letter in her head.

My sister had left her post as a nanny and was now working in London. With our moving to Portsmouth we would see even less of her and would have to rely more on correspondence or the odd expensive telephone call and perhaps an occasional visit.

Our exploration of the house, at least for the time being, was complete. The removal men were on the point of leaving and Bert had returned from his reconnoitring to lend a hand with the work load. Mother made a pot of tea and on cue our new landlord suddenly appeared.

Mr. Elliot was a big man, ex-army, and still retaining much of his military bearing. He had a large red face, thinning hair and a drooping moustache, once ginger but now drained of most of its original colour. In future weeks he would become a regular visitor.

Without fail he would arrive punctually on a Monday morning – Mother's wash day – to collect the rent. He would seat himself down at one end of the living room table, with Mother opposite, and over a cup of tea he would proceed to put the world to rights. (Not an easy task in these days!) Sometimes Mother would share with him her simple faith, and he would often say that he left a better man for talking with her.

Eventually my much used wooden brick-box was located and I was despatched to the garden to play on my own.

The garden was much smaller, regimental and restrictive. Sadly no trains ran at the bottom of it, there seemed no place to dig, and the old galvanised bath that had once been home to my crocodile would have now seemed somehow out of place. On one side was a high brick wall with a large blackberry bush clinging to it. There were flowers everywhere A rose bush, not yet in bloom, climbed over a rustic awning and hung across the back wall. Other flowers bordered the lawn while three large circular beds filled with red and yellow tulips punctuated it. A host of tiny blue flowers (*Campanula*) edged the narrow path that led up to the garden door.

This door was the most exciting discovery of all. On the other side of it lay a network of narrow alleyways that continued over the roads on both sides of our block. In the months ahead it would provide a perfect play venue for cowboys and Indians; war games; hide and seek; kick-the-ball-trot, and many more!

At last I found an area of the lawn to play on. I emptied my brick-box on to the neatly cut grass and began to build. Usually my buildings were more ambitious. I had often spend hours building houses, theatres or cathedrals. This time I chose to make the outline of a ship. It took most of my bricks, and when it was completed I sat inside it pretending I was the captain, sailing across a vast green sea.

Suddenly I became aware of someone watching me. I turned quickly and was just in time to see a face disappearing behind the high brick wall. Minutes later it reappeared. It was the face of a little girl.

For a long time we stared at each other. The girl was older than me, perhaps by a year. She had a shock of red hair, green-grey eyes, and was covered in freckles. At last she broke the silence.

'What's that?' she asked, pointing to my wooden bricks.

'It's a ship,' I replied. She wrinkled her nose and looked unimpressed.

'Where have you come from?'

'A long way,' I said.

'*How* long?' She must have been standing on a ladder for as she raised herself higher I could see the top of her dress.

'This *long?*' she asked, and she extended both arms wide.

'No, *this long!*' I stretched out my arms to their fullest extent. She looked in disbelief.

'What's your name?' she asked. I told her.

'My name's Brenda,' she said.

And so began a very special wartime friendship.

Five

Brenda

IN THE SUMMER MONTHS that followed, Brenda and I were inseparable. We played, argued, ran errands, went on outings and sometimes when the air raids started and became heavier we shared the same bed.

The first time we played together was in Brenda's back garden. Almost at once we were involved in a fierce and noisy argument, which left Brenda in tears and running down the path to her mother.

'He pinched me!' she cried. 'He pinched me!'

I stood there, guilty and ashamed; trying desperately to hide behind the apple tree and feeling like a younger Adam about to be expelled from the Garden of Eden. Fortunately, Mrs Webber, Brenda's mother, had mercy on me! She promptly intervened and sent us both in doors to play a *'quiet game.'* The tears soon turned to laughter and somehow our friendship began to blossom. We became closer than ever.

I suppose, because Brenda was older, and perhaps a little more dominant, we tended to play mostly girl's games:, *mothers and fathers, schools and hospitals.* Usually these involved Brenda's dolls and, sometimes my long suffering bear, now sadly a little worse for wear with both of his glass eyes missing; replaced by two of Mother's press-studs.

There was always a strong sense of competition between us. When we sat on the old garden table with our little legs dangling over it, dipping our clay pipes into the bowl of bubble mixture beside us, it was to see who could blow the biggest bubbles, or the bubble that would float the furthest, or simply the bubble that would outlast all the others!

Then there was the *sweets* ritual – which of us could make our sweets last the longest. Choosing sweets became a serious business! As soon as we had received our pocket money we would run to the corner shop and carefully scrutinise every sweet jar on the shelves.

Mrs. Legg, who owned the sweet shop, was not exactly known for her patience, especially when dealing with indecisive little children. The longer we deliberated the more visibly agitated she became.

'Now which is it to be?' she would ask; her hands hovering over the sweet jars. 'Hurry up and make up your minds!'

But Brenda stubbornly refused to be hurried for although sweets were still unrationed [4] our pocket money wasn't. After much consideration and further conferring the final choice was made and Mrs. Legg, thankfully, shovelled our selections into little white paper bags, and then watched as we departed from the shop running down the road, up the alleyway, and back home.

Once indoors we would slowly open the bags and even more slowly begin to devour their contents. But however hard Brenda tried, and much to her annoyance, it was almost always her sweets that disappeared first.

By now our parents were becoming increasingly friendly, especially Mother and Mrs. Webber *(Louie)*. We saw less of Mr. Webber; he was a manager of the furniture department in the big Fratton Road Co-op. He was a quiet, thoughtful man who found the war very disturbing and was becoming more and more depressed by the worsening situation.

One afternoon it was decided we would visit the sea front – a bus ride away. Usually the promenade would be thronged with people but today it was strangely deserted. Instead coils of barbed wire stretched across its entire length blocking access to the beach and sea, and although Dad lifted me high on his shoulders it

---

[4] Sweet rationing commenced July 26th 1942 and ended February 5th 1953

was impossible to see what lay beyond, but Brenda said she thought she could see *something!*

Eventually we crossed over the road and made our way to the Canoe Lake. On a normal day, with the sun shining as it was, the grounds of the Canoe Lake would have been filled with people, young and old, families and friends, carefree couples and children playing by the water's edge, some with small sailing boats trailing behind them.

And on the lake itself there would have been the hire-boats – colourful canoes, rowing boats and paddle boats, all splashing their way through the water, while the man with the megaphone would have called in the numbers:

'Seven . . . Come in number seven!' 'Twenty-four . . . Your time is up!'

Now all was quiet. The boats were nowhere to be seen and, except for a handful of people and a few squawking seagulls, we had the lake to ourselves.

Our parents had stopped and were engaged in conversation. I went on ahead while Brenda stayed within earshot. It was obvious they would be discussing the war; the grown-ups seemed to talk about little else, indeed there was much to talk about – Mr. Churchill, the new Prime Minister; the miraculous evacuation of Dunkirk; the fall of France and with it the very real and frightening threat of imminent invasion.

War for me meant *sailors and soldiers in smart uniforms.*

Airman and aeroplanes; sandbags, barrage balloons and the blackout, (and no bananas!) Up until now I had been cocooned from much of the horror and awfulness of war.

Eventually Brenda caught up with me. She seemed strangely quiet and withdrawn.

'What's the matter?' I asked.

She shook her head and then, very softly said: 'I wish there wasn't a war.' And then vehemently: 'I hate Hitler!'

I said: 'Silly old Hitler!' The day was too nice to spoil and I said it again, louder this time: *'Silly old Hitler!'* And then we began to call him all the names we could think of. We made up songs and pulled funny faces; we laughed and began to jump up and down. We made so much noise we were told to quieten down.

Certainly Hitler was not amused! On the eleventh day of July he vented his wrath upon Portsmouth. The Luftwaffe struck for the first time and bombs rained down on the northern part of the city. Two hotels were hit, a gas-holder pierced and set on fire. Houses were demolished and there was a direct hit on a school. Altogether that evening eighteen people were killed and eighty injured.

On another occasion, this time an early evening, we went to Fratton Park, the home of Pompey Football Club. It was not to see a football match however, (that would come much later), but to see a combined demonstration staged by the Civil Defence, St. John Ambulance Brigade and the Fire Service.

The highlight and culmination of the evening was a pre-fabricated house quickly set up in the middle of the pitch, a mock explosion followed. The house burst into flames, smoke poured from its windows and the Fire Brigade sprang into action. Hoses were rolled out, jets of water were sprayed on to the flames, a body was stretchered from the smoking building and soon the fire was out and everything under control. A burst of spontaneous applause echoed around the ground. The band played and the crowd was dismissed.

The last of the sunlight still lingered and illuminated the green turf as we made our way from the terraces and hurried home. Our imaginations were fired. I had wanted to be an engine driver, and a dustman, then a postman. Now I had to be a fireman.

If we could just reach home in time we might be able to put on a fire display of our own. Brenda pointed out that we didn't even possess a hose, but then I remembered that we kept a large brass garden syringe in a bucket in the conservatory. It was usually there for watering plants and mother also used it as a deterrent to the numerous cats that found their way into our garden. It would certainly make a good fire extinguisher.

It was not to be. The light was failing fast; dusk was

already descending. Our plans would have to wait for another day, in any case Brenda's mother had invited us all back to her house for refreshments.

While our parents chatted Brenda and I discussed what we should do.

'Let's explore upstairs.' Brenda suggested. And together we quietly slid away from our parents.

Because the top of the house was not completely light-proof it meant finding our way in the dark. With the stringent rules governing the blackout and the ever diligent wardens ready to enforce them with shouts of: *'Put out those LIGHTS!'* and even a possible fine, it meant carefully using Brenda's torch for illumination. The pocket torch had now become a very important item. Both Brenda and I had become very attached to our little *Ever-ready torches.*

Once when night had just fallen, as a special treat we were allowed out into the darkness, carrying our torches, to run the entire length of the alleyways in our slippered feet! A few minutes and we were home again, completely out of breath and our hearts racing after such an exciting adventure!

Now Brenda led the way upstairs, the beam from her torch suddenly fastening on furniture and other objects, throwing strange and grotesque shadows across the room and landing. It was quiet and eerie. The voices downstairs became indistinct and seemed far away. Suddenly we both felt a sense of fear and panic and quickly fled down the stairs to the lighted rooms below.

Our mothers were in the kitchen while the two men were deep in conversation. Mr. Webber looked strained, even melancholic. Dad was worried about him. Later, when we were home, he shared with Mother his concern.

'Poor chap,' he said. 'He sees no hope for the future.'

As the year wore on the air raids became heavier, with more destruction, death and casualties. In the August the 'Battle of Britain' raged across the skies; by September it was over, the gallant RAF had won through. On September 7th the blitz commenced with intensified bombing of many of our major cities including our own. I was now five years old.

In December we celebrated another Christmas. Somehow Mother managed to find us a tree and Bert began the task of decorating the home. On Christmas Eve, Brenda and I were so excited we couldn't sleep. Mrs. Webber even allowed Brenda out of her bed to show me her empty pillowcase that she was hoping Father Christmas would fill. I wondered if perhaps I should have chosen a pillowcase instead of a stocking.

In the morning we both discovered that, despite the on-going war, Father Christmas had still managed a visit and we all celebrated another Christmas.

New Years Eve quickly followed and we all wondered what the new year would bring. I was now seeing less of Brenda for she had already started school and found that she really loved it. I would have to wait until September but I was in no hurry for school to begin.

One morning there was loud knocking at our front door; Brenda and her mother stood outside. They looked distraught and in a state of shock. Brenda was crying. Something had happened; something very serious, but I was unaware just how serious. Dad, Mother and Bert all went away with Mrs. Webber, leaving Brenda to stay with me.

She came into the living room and lay back on the old couch in the corner. Her face was very pale; there were dark circles under her eyes and her red hair looked even darker. Usually when Brenda was sad I could always make her laugh; this time it was different. No matter how hard I tried, and however ridiculous my antics, they drew no response. Once a glimmer of a smile passed her lips but vanished almost immediately. At last she spoke, so quietly I could barely hear what she had to say.

'I'll never see my Daddy again.' She said.

Months of mounting anxiety and fear had taken their toll. Perhaps the terrible incendiary raid in January had been the turning point, it was on that night the store where Mr. Webber worked, the huge Fratton Road Co-op, had been set ablaze leaving only its outer walls intact. In a fit of depression Brenda's father had tragically taken his own life.. He was, after all, just another unrecorded casualty of war.

After the funeral Brenda and her mother went to the Isle of Wight to stay for a short while with relations. Mother and I went with them on to the Harbour Station, there was just time to watch the "Mud Larks," boys and girls from the Portsea area who waded and performed in the mud flats, covered in mud, some up to their knees in it, scrambling for coins thrown down by the many laughing onlookers.

Brenda and I both threw some pennies and then quickly made our way to the jetty below. where we said our goodbyes waving as they crossed the gang plank to board the waiting ferry. Smoke belched out from the steamer's funnel and the two giant paddles slowly began to turn, threshing the water into a white foam, and leaving a trail behind them. Once more we waved until the paddle steamer was almost out of sight and then we made our way home.

Mrs. Webber, now a widow, needed work to support both herself and her daughter. Later that year Brenda and her mother moved away from Portsmouth to begin a new life in the little Sussex seaside resort of Shoreham. Sadly we said our goodbyes.

Six

Hilda

IT IS STILL A MYSTERY as to why and when Hilda suddenly decided to leave Reigate and make her home in Portsmouth. Not only had Hilda been our next door neighbour in Doods Road, she was also Mother's best friend.

She was perhaps a few years younger than mother; in her early forties, slightly built, with light brown permed hair, always neatly dressed and seldom without a friendly smile. She had never married and, as far as I knew, had lived most of her life with her father, old Mister Chamberlain, in his house next door to us in Doods Road.

On a wash-day, when pegging out the clothes, Mother would see Hilda's head suddenly appear over the garden hedge. Down would go the washing basket and both Mother and Hilda would become engaged in animated chatter.

Sometimes while they were talking I would creep up behind Mother and untie her apron strings.

'Why you little pickle!' she would exclaim, then laughing and turning to Hilda she would continue: 'Well, this won't do, we'd better get on or we'll never get finished!'

Now it was no longer a hedge that separated us but several roads. Hilda had moved to a house in Mayles Road, the very last road off our own Warren Avenue. Beyond this lay the asylum, then the farm with its pungent pig smell and the Creek with its colourful assortment of houseboats permanently moored to the muddy shoreline, some with their own little gardens. But the extra distance separating our houses had in no way lessened our involvement with Hilda.

Often she would pop in for a chat. 'Just passing!' she would say, and on would go the kettle and Mother and Hilda would happily catch up with each other's news. Both had much in common. They loved needlework and dressmaking, while Hilda's speciality was button making. Neither could resist a bargain!

In our early exploratory days in Portsmouth it was Hilda who organized our shopping expeditions. There were four main shopping centres, Commercial Road, Southsea, Fratton Road and North End and besides these several smaller shopping areas.

After Reigate the Portsmouth shops looked huge

and to me, just counter-top high, they seemed to stretch for miles! Some were two storeys high and others even three. Each shop seemed to have its share of customers all intent on making a purchase, and seemingly oblivious to the on-going war.

That was about to change. Sadly within months of our visits all that would remain of these very same shops would be blackened, burnt-out shells, piled up bricks and twisted red-rusted girders.

But it would not be just the shopping trips and other outings with Hilda that I would remember but one special event . . . the day when I fell in love with the gramophone . . .

The first time I saw a wind-up gramophone was at a jumble sale. Mother loved jumble sales. Dad often said that she had a real knack, as he called it, for finding a bargain. The hall was already open and when we arrived the sale had already begun. Outside an old man cranked at the handle of a barrel-organ while a chained monkey, wearing a fez and ruff, performed for him. Inside it was crowded, noisy and hot. Close to the entrance, and on one of the tables, stood a little portable wind-up gramophone.

The wooden lid was open, the chrome arm and attached sound box gleamed as the light caught it. A tiny shellac record with a bright red label was placed on the green-beige covered turntable. The arm was lowered and the needle slid into the groove of the record.

Slowly the turntable began to revolve, there was a loud hiss followed by crackles, and then a man began to sing, his metallic voice rising high above the noise in the hall . . .

"Lazy Mary, will you get up?
   Will you get up, will you get up?
 Lazy Mary will you get up on a fine and frosty morning?"
"What have I got for my breakfast, my breakfast, my breakfast? . . . .
What have I got for my breakfast?
   On a fine and frosty morning?"[5]

There were a few more turns of the handle, and the voice became higher and the music faster.

"No Mother I won't get up, I won't get up, I won't get up . . ."

It seemed nothing would entice lazy Mary to get up for her breakfast until she was promised: *"A nice young man with rosy cheeks."*

---

[5] This was one of the records in the collection. Certainly one I remember clearly and one most often played

"Yes mother, I will get up. I will get up; I will get up, on a fine and frosty morning!"

I stood there transfixed. I begged Mother to buy this wonderful gramophone and the records that went with it, and for a moment she seemed to hesitate.

'Whatever will your Daddy say?' She seemed to address the question to herself rather than to me.

I pleaded with her but to no avail. Reluctantly, dragging my feet, I followed her around the other stalls until I could no longer hear the music.

At last it was time to go. As we were leaving we were met by Hilda and soon she and Mother were laughing and chatting. Mother must have told her about the gramophone, and I'm not sure what Hilda said to her, but suddenly there we were back in the hall, and when we emerged we were carrying the gramophone and the case full of records!

I will always be grateful to Hilda for I'm quite sure it was her intervention on that day long ago that was responsible for my Mother's change of heart and my ongoing love affair with the gramophone.

Seven

The Evacuees

MOTHER PUTS A MATCH TO THE FIRE *then disappears into the kitchen where she begins to prepare the evening meal. We've just come back from shopping and I'm sitting in my fold-up carpet chair watching and daydreaming as the smoke and orange flames mingle together sending shadows dancing across the living room walls and ceiling. The black coals glow red and odd changing shapes and faces begin to appear.*

As the fire settles so the steady tick-tock, tick-tock from the mantle-piece clock becomes louder and more insistent. This small rosewood clock standing on its four wooden pillars suddenly reminds me of another time when its shiny brass pendulum swung from side to side above another mantle-piece in another room − my Reigate living-room . . .

I lay on the living room couch, propped up with pillows, in an improvised bed. Beside me were books, bottles of medicine, and a glass thermometer which protruded out of a large tumbler of water.

The fire glowed in the grate, the flames looking anaemic in the sunlit room, but suddenly brightening as another cloud passed across the sun, darkening the room, and sending a flurry of snowflakes to add to the already thick layer of snow covering the garden and beyond.

I pulled the blankets up higher and hugged my teddy bear tightly towards me. This little plump bear had been a present from my sister, Renie. At first I had flatly rejected him, but in my fever, I had called for him again, and now we were becoming great friends. In the war years that lay ahead we were to become almost inseparable. Wearing his own tin hat and knitted scarf, he would accompany me through the 'blitz' while we took refuge under the stairs, and later in the air raid shelter, where he would be a comfort to me as the bombs screamed down from overhead.

Once more I looked out through the living room window. *'If only I could go out,'* I thought. But the doctor had given strict instructions to Mother: 'Whatever you do, keep him in bed and keep him warm!'

My brother had already been out in the garden, his deep footprints now almost obliterated by fresh falls of snow. He had braved the cold to make me a magnificent snowman, resplendent in my Father's old trilby hat and scarf.

The snowman sat there, cross-legged on an old fallen tree trunk, staring back at me with coal-black impassive eyes and a clay pipe that drooped from under his carrot nose.

Mother had just slipped out to do some shopping leaving me with the two evacuees, a brother and sister who had come to stay with us. They had arrived shortly after the outbreak of war. Mother had opened the front door to find a very harassed lady standing outside with two young children.

Both the children looked tired and apprehensive, each carrying a small suitcase while over their shoulders hung the mandatory gas-masks and pinned to their overcoats were their name-tags. The lady with them seemed only too anxious that they be taken off her hands as quickly as possible and was relieved when Mother agreed they could stay with us. The lady promised to call back later leaving Mother to gently shepherd the children inside the house.

'Now don't you worry,' Mother had reassured them, 'after you've had some tea you can tell us all about yourselves and where you've come from.'

And that evening, when we were all together, they did. In a short while they had settled in with us, and for a time they became a very real part of our family.

The girl was bright eyed, excitable, (a little 'chatterbox,' Mother had called her) and sometimes she was given to wild exaggerations. The boy was a little older, taller, quieter and very protective towards his younger sister.

They now both came into the room giggling. The girl waving a duster in her hand began to polish the living room furniture. Standing on tip-toe she stretched to reach the mantelpiece and was dusting the clock when, suddenly and without warning, she burst into tears. She cried quietly at first but then with uncontrollable sobs.

The boy put his arms around her. 'Don't cry,' he said with concern. 'Please tell me what's wrong.' But all she would say, through giant sobs, was: 'I want to go home!' over and over again, 'I want to go home!'

From my makeshift bed I also tried to console her only to be ignored.

It was at this point that Mother had returned. Quickly putting the shopping down she lovingly smothered the little girl in her arms.

'Whatever's the matter?' she asked. 'Whatever's all this noise about?'

At last the sobs subsided, and after some deep breaths the girl managed to speak.

'I've broken your lovely clock.' she wept.

Apparently, whilst dusting the mantel-piece clock, she had somehow managed to dislodge the swinging brass pendulum and seeing it lying disengaged beside the clock she immediately thought she had broken it.

Mother laughed. 'Is that all it is!' she said, and then

picking up the pendulum she deftly re-hinged it back in position bringing the clock back to life with its warm distinctive *tick-tock! tick-tock!*

'There! It's not broken at all.' Mother reassured her. 'And even if it were,' she continued. 'It wouldn't be the end of the world, now would it?'

With her arm still around the little girl she led her off to the scullery and began to prepare the dinner. Soon laughter rang out from the back of the house.

I snuggled deeper into the blankets. And the sun came out once more.

* * *

I wonder what happened to the evacuees. I can't even remember their names now. Perhaps they are back in their own London home or once again evacuated to a new home in the country. I doubt that I shall ever know but, while I sit warm and secure by the fire with the clock above still ticking, and Mother in the kitchen, softly singing, I think how lucky I am, and despite the air-raids and the bombs that terrify me, I'm so glad not to be an evacuee.

Eight

School Days

I AM ON THE EDGE OF THE PAVEMENT *surrounded by people. A cavalcade of cars make their way in slow procession along the roadway. The crowd are noisy and ecstatic; they wave and cheer. One of the cars slows and stops directly beside me. With a shock I recognise the occupant.*

It is Adolf Hitler.

I can clearly see his Charlie Chaplin moustache and, from under the rim of his peaked cap, his piercing black eyes look straight through me. Suddenly he is out of the car; his heavy jack boots hit the pavement; he strides towards me. An arm, bearing an ugly black swastika, is reaching out to grab me. I start to run, but my legs are as lead, they refuse to move; at any moment I shall feel his hand upon my shoulder. I glance behind me and to my surprise Hitler is nowhere to be seen, in his place is another pursuer—my school teacher! I can see her thin, red lipstick lips, moving and a bright red tipped finger points directly towards

51

me . . . .I try to shout . . .
  Mummy! Mummy! Mummy!

  'David! Wake up! Wake up; you're dreaming!'
Mother stands by my bed and wipes my damp
forehead. 'It's just a dream,' she says. 'You've been
dreaming!'

My first day at school

My early school days were not always the happiest
ones of my life! They began when I first put on my
blazer and tie and with my gas mask case over my
shoulder, walked beside my mother the short distance
from home to school – Meon Road Infants.

When we arrived the playground was full of
children. A teacher emerged from one of the doors
and began to ring the school bell vigorously. With a
mixture of apprehension and expectancy we
disentangled ourselves from our mothers, waved our
"goodbyes" and were ushered into a large hall and
then to one of the many classrooms.

Each of us were assigned our own desks and we sat
at them stiffly, taking stock of our new surroundings.
Many of us were close to tears yet determined not to
cry. It was as though we had suffered an amputation. A
huge chunk of our freedom seemed to have been

severed from us and somehow we knew life would never be quite the same again.

Our teacher, who stood at the front of the class, holding a long white pointer, seemed pleasant enough and tried to reassure us. After some necessary formalities we were given some plasticine and allowed to choose and shape any object we chose. Then there came a visit by the headmistress.

'Right children, you know what to say.' This was an earlier rehearsed moment. 'All together now!'

'Good morning, Head Mistress.'

The headmistress responded. 'Good morning, children.'

She seemed faintly amused as she studied our intense faces. She was a small woman, slightly built yet conveying great presence and authority. She looked at us with all-seeing eyes and gave us a no-nonsense smile. After welcoming us to the school she proceeded, with our teacher, to take a walk around the classroom, stopping at each desk to appraise or make a comment. Once her tour over we were told, each in turn, to call out our name and birthday.

'David Jupp. My birthday is on the twelfth of September, Headmistress.'

A few desks behind me in the same row was another boy who also had the same birthday.

'George Paste. My birthday is the twelfth of September.'

'There,' she said, seizing on this apparent

coincidence. 'You two boys must be twins!' and looking around the class she questioned. 'Who can tell me what twins are?'

*   *   *

And so the day wore on, in reality it only lasted a few hours, but it seemed for ever. At last the school bell rang and we were dismissed to join our anxious waiting parents. Our first day at school was over, but only to be repeated the next day and the next, and the next week, and the next month, until all the days, weeks and months merged together to become years. Our faltering journey into education had begun. We were under a new discipline where the teacher was our authority and criteria. The facts, figures and formulae that she wrote on the blackboard with her squeaky white chalk and all that she taught us must surely be true. I was now able to tell my less enlightened parents that we had all come from monkeys!

'Who ever told you that?' they asked.

'My teacher,' I replied.

*   *   *

Of course, school was not all bad. As well as arithmetic and those terrible times-tables that had to be repeated over and over again, there were also good things: playtimes, stories, games and PT, this would usually be followed by *O'Grady Says.*[6] My favourite lessons were   art and craft. I also had my favourite teachers, and besides constant skirmishes with the bullies there were also real friendships to be made. One of these was with a new boy named Brian.

Brian

The school term had already begun when Brian joined us. I believe he and his Mother had recently moved to Portsmouth as his father was an officer serving in the Royal Navy. Brian was possessed by a boundless pent up energy that uncaged itself in the playground. The two most popular games at this time were "aeroplanes" and "steam trains." To be an "aeroplane," besides making the appropriate sounds, you had to stretch both arms out as wings and weave, circle and attack other "enemy aircraft!" Brian was unstoppable.

To play "steam trains" it was necessary to become an "engine," emitting engine noises and moving each arm alternatively backwards and forwards to simulate the action of the train. Other children would then

---

[6] Often called 'Simon Says.' If we were caught doing an action that O'Grady had not said then we were disqualified

endeavour to join and follow the "engine" as "carriages."

Brian would simply roar around the playground in ever increasing circles; any would-be "carriages" trying to fasten on to him would quickly be derailed. For me this became a challenge. I would watch him from the edge of the playground, his compact frame straining forward, animated yet totally absorbed and in a world of his own. He was completely oblivious to the rest of us. If no one else could keep up with him, then I determined that I would.

One playtime with Brian at full steam, I decided to launch myself on to him. I seized just the right moment and became his one and only "carriage." When the bell rang for lessons I was still there behind him. This was repeated over successive days. Neither of us spoke. Then about the third day Brian suddenly slowed and stopped running, he turned and faced me and the silence was broken. From that moment we became friends.

Like many of the boys, Brian would sometimes use the odd swear word. In my own rather sheltered upbringing I had never been exposed to any bad language. The nearest my Father came to swearing was to use the word *bloomin'* and this he only found necessary when relating to the neighbour's cockerel, hell bent on waking him up on a Sunday morning; or else the persistent barking of a neighbourhood dog.

At school I was constantly bombarded with expletives that I found both disturbing and distressing. At night I would lie in bed and hear those same words running through my head, over and over again.

One morning in the playground I spoke to Brian. 'Brian,' I said. 'When you swear it's not just me who hears you, there's someone else.'

Brian looked thoughtful. 'Who's that?' he asked.

'It's Jesus.' I told him. I hope I didn't sound too pious. I didn't mean to, for I was certainly no saint. To my surprise Brian seemed greatly impressed, he seized the nearest boy to him and to my embarrassment made me repeat what I had just said all over again. As far as I can remember I never heard Brian swear again.

Over the months that followed we became great friends both in and out of school. We played in each other's houses, made up elaborate war games and went to each other's birthday parties. One lunch time Brian invited me back to meet his father, who had just come home on a short leave and was still unpacking.

'My Dad's got something for you.' Brian told me.

At this point Brian's father disappeared upstairs only to return moments later with, what to me was worth more than gold. *Two green bananas!* One he gave to Brian, the other to me. I now held in my hand a *real live banana.* I think it was the first one I had seen since the war began. I raced home to show my Mother and then waited patiently for it to ripen.

Brian and I remained great friends until he was eventually sent to a new school; this was almost at the end of the war. After that, like so many other school friends, we lost touch.

The Prize

Every morning, after the register had been called and marked, we all trooped into the hall for assembly. Our headmistress was already standing on her podium. One look was sufficient to bring order out of chaos. We took our places hardly daring to breath. On this particular morning I was startled to hear my own name being called.

'*David Jupp*, will you please come to the front of the hall.'

It took several moments before it registered with me. The headmistress repeated herself.

'Is *David Jupp* there? Yes, I can see him!' Come to the front of the hall.'

With fear and trembling I began to make my way past the other children to stand by the small platform. A teacher struck a chord on the piano and the children began to sing the chosen morning hymn. Standing at the front and facing them I was surprised how loud it all sounded. I was now feeling very apprehensive.

Fearing the worst I began searching my head for any misdemeanour I might have committed. One of the teachers standing on the platform smiled down at me giving me a reassuring nod and then the headmistress, herself, mouthed that I need not look so worried as there was nothing for me to worry about. That was a relief anyway!

At the conclusion of the hymn all the children were motioned to sit on the floor. I remained standing feeling exposed and very vulnerable as at least one hundred and fifty pairs of eyes stared up at me.

The headmistress spoke: 'Some time ago,' she began, 'this school and other schools in our city entered a competition to promote *National Savings* contributions . . .'

I had all but forgotten and now I suddenly remembered. Months ago I had drawn and crayoned a picture of aeroplanes flying low over stubby trees with their guns firing, bombs exploding and pilots parachuting to safety. And across it I had written the slogan: 'SAVE FOR VICTORY!'

The headmistress was still speaking: 'And I'm pleased to tell you that David Jupp has won, for himself and the school, a *Third Prize*. Well done, David.'

My reward was a two shillings and sixpenny Savings stamp, bright red, the same colour as my face.

'All together now children . . . *Hip, hip* . . . *Hooray!* And again . . . Hip, hip . . . . .'

As the cheers rang out I quickly moved back to my place. I was still dazed, juggling with a mixture of feelings: relief, embarrassment and just a little pride. One teacher told me she had seen my name printed in the local paper, the *Evening News*, and if I wanted to see my picture and the other prize winning entrees, they would be on display in the window of 'Whites' the big furniture shop which was situated on the main London Road on the corner of Stubbington Avenue.

Later one evening, together with my Mother and Father, we caught the bus to North End to see it displayed with the other entries in the shop window. When the picture was eventually returned to me it was placed in a prominent position on the bureau in our front room and there it remained for a considerable time until it finally disappeared for ever.

When we had reached the age of seven we were no longer infants but had moved on to the junior school. This was, in fact, a part of the same building but we now had a headmaster – Mr. Williams, and there were new teachers and a bigger playground. We were, for the first time, completely segregated from the girls except when there was an air raid. Now we were with the "big boys". We played football, marbles and flew paper aeroplanes. We formed and joined gangs and sometimes had fights in the playground.

In our new classrooms we used pens and ink to

write with. The pens had plain wooden handles and steel nibs and these were handed out each morning, and each desk was equipped with a small white china inkwell. It could be messy! The steel nibs were also very easy to damage.

'There are too many of you children who are not looking after your pens properly,' accused a stern-faced teacher. 'It is simply carelessness and it's got to *STOP.* If I find anyone damaging a pen they're going to be in *TROUBLE!'* And she meant it.

Not very long after this warning my pen had found its way on to the classroom floor! I watched in dismay, as it fell, nib down, almost in slow motion, down on to the wooden floor. Quickly, in fear and trepidation, I bent down to retrieve it and found to my horror the pen nib badly buckled and completely beyond repair. Making sure no one was watching I carefully slid it under my jumper, took it home and guiltily buried it at the bottom of my garden where, as far as I know, it still remains to this day.

A Belated Achievement

In the upper school the work was much harder. I had found arithmetic difficult enough in the *Infants*, now it became a daily struggle. Worse still was my total inability to read. It had already caused me embarrassment. Once I had been sent with a message to the Headmaster's office where, without hesitation, I had opened the door and walked boldly in to discover the headmaster in conversation with an important looking visitor. My intrusion was not welcomed!

'Go outside again and when you've read the notice on the door you can do what it says.'

For a long time I waited outside staring at the door until it was opened once more this time by the headmaster. At last, realising I was unable to read, he read the notice for me: 'KNOCK AND WAIT. Now let's try that again.' he said. 'And remember you must never, ever, enter my office without first knocking.'

I left the office flushed and deeply shamed. I was determined to tell no one. However word got around.

'I hope,' said my teacher, and she seemed to be looking in my direction. 'I *hope* that the rude little boy that burst into the headmaster's office without knocking was not anyone in this class.'

I *hoped* I was invisible.

The teacher who took us for reading was Mrs. Lovett. She was one of the younger teachers and perhaps not as understanding as I would have liked. In turn she cajoled, encouraged, and even bullied me without success. Every reading lesson, which I had begun to dread, she would hand out our books and we would each in turn be expected to read two or three sentences.

I would sit there desperately trying to make sense of

the printed words which only seemed to mock me. When it came to my turn nothing would come. I stood up mumbled some incoherent sounds and then deadly silence. Mrs. Lovett would stare at me from across the classroom, her thin pencilled eyebrows arched in frustration.

'You *must* try' she said sharply. 'You must try *much* harder.'

But the more I tried the more impossible it became. I began to have nightmares. My Mother worried over me and even went to the school to talk to the teacher, while my brother spent hours trying to help me, all to no avail. The words simply didn't mean anything.

Then one unforgettable afternoon, almost as if in a dream, I suddenly heard myself reading aloud.

'He's reading!' she cried, and she quickly moved from her desk towards me. 'You can read!' And her face was all smiles. 'No don't stop. Listen children, he can read.'

Not only was I reading, but I was reading with expression and intonation. The words simply flowed.

A week later I was standing on the stage in the big hall where I had been chosen as one of the narrators for the end-of-term school play. As I looked down at the sea of faces I caught sight of the headmaster and Mrs. Lovett seated in the front row. They were laughing and chatting, a red tipped finger pointed in my direction and I knew that I was the subject of their conversation. I wondered what they were saying . . .

*So this is the boy who burst into my office without knocking!
The boy we never thought would learn to read.*
Oh, I always knew he would, headmaster, I always knew!

I allowed her to share in my triumph. The lights dimmed, the hall hushed, I took a deep breath and began my narration.

Nine

Air Raids

ONE MORNING DURING A SCHOOL LESSON the air raid siren sounded.

'Right, children, you all know what to do! Have you all got your gas masks?'

We felt a momentary sense of panic as we left our desks and headed for the corridor. The siren was still wailing as other classes emptied and joined us to be herded together towards the school shelter.

'Not so much noise!' A teacher shouted above the din. 'Quieten down now!'

At last we converged upon the shelter, which was in reality a converted cloakroom, specially reinforced to provide some degree of safety. While we were standing outside its entrance waiting for the congestion to ease, one of the girls from another class said something that shocked us all. With quiet conviction she told us:

'I love Hitler.'

We stared at her aghast. For a few moments the air raid was forgotten.

'Ugh!' said the big girl standing beside me. 'Hitler's horrible. You can't love Hitler!'

'I think Hitler's nice,' said the first girl quite unrepentant.

'Hurry up now!' shouted the teacher. 'Move along.'

The big girl tried desperately to attract his attention.

'Please, sir! Please, sir! *She,*' pointing to the girl in question. '*She* said she loves Hitler.'

'Come on now. No more talking.'

If he heard what she said he chose to ignore it. After all he did have more important matters to consider – our safety.

At last we were all ushered inside and accounted for. As we sat on the wooden benches, waiting for the planes to come and the bombs to fall, I suddenly became very anxious. I wanted to be at home with my mother. What if a bomb fell on our house? I might never see my Mother again. What if a bomb fell on the school? What if . . . ?

At this point my thoughts were suddenly interrupted. The 'all-clear' sounded; the air raid, after all, had not materialised. Perhaps it had been a false alarm, or perhaps the enemy raiders had by-passed Portsmouth and were even now heading towards another target.

Back in the classroom it was difficult to settle down. I could still hear that little girl's voice in my head:

'I love Hitler.' *And* 'I think he's nice.'

It was hard to understand how anyone could love or admire someone who was responsible for so much devastation and suffering. *(Perhaps it was only her gratitude for the interruption to the lesson.)* The bell rang for lunch. I ran through the school gates to find Mother waiting for me.

When the air raids began we were without a shelter. This may have been due to a general shortage or the reluctance on the part of our landlord, Mr. Elliot, to have his beautiful garden dug up and desecrated.

A Daylight raid

Our nearest public communal shelter was in Milton Park. We used it only once, and that was during a very heavy daylight raid.

Earlier Mother and I had caught the bus to Hilsea Lido. The swimming pool was closed and barricaded with barbed wire but the boating lake and surrounding grounds were still accessible although mostly deserted. We crossed over the picturesque wooden bridge that spanned the lake and climbed the far embankment and began our explorations.

This was not the only time we had visited the lido, in-fact it was one of the few places Dad had taken us when we first came to Portsmouth. It had been a Sunday evening and as now was quite deserted. We had walked beside the lake with Bert in the lead. Suddenly he had moved even closer to the water's edge. Dad shouted a warning:

'I should come away from there if I were you. You're much too near the edge! We don't want you falling in!'

For some reason my brother, ignoring his father's advice, had stepped on to a patch of green slippery slime and the next moment there had been, a tremendous splash. My brother had disappeared into the lake to emerge seconds later, unhurt but thoroughly soaked, smelling to "high heaven" and his best Sunday suit ruined. To add further to his embarrassment, Bert had boarded the bus for home and found himself sitting close to one of his work colleagues from the Airspeed factory. Dad could not suppress a chuckle.

It was now getting late in the afternoon.

'I think it's time for us to go.' Mother said.

We left the lido, caught the bus and had almost reached our home when the siren sounded. There had been spasmodic gun-fire earlier but this was the real thing. Our bus driver ignored our stop and pulled up outside the park and as quickly as we could we all made our way to the shelter. A warden waited to usher us inside.

It was a dismal place, damp, dimly lit, crowded and claustrophobic. We manoeuvred our way past the other bodies and eventually found a seat near the rear of the shelter. The lady sitting next to my Mother soon realized she had a captive listener and began to pour out her troubles. Meanwhile a small group of people to the front of us tried to lift our spirits with a half-hearted rendition of one of the popular songs of the day.

Outside, up in the sky above us, the battle raged. We could hear the dull drones of the German bombers and the whines of their accompanying fighter planes plus the barrage of heavy anti-aircraft gunfire, followed by shrill whistles and awful thuds as the bombs fell and exploded on and around their targets.

The noise from the bombardment grew louder and more intense and then suddenly subsided and the 'all-clear' sounded, and it was all over. Thankfully we made our way out into the sunshine, took a deep breath and headed for home.

Later that evening the raiders came again, circling above us. Their attack concentrating mainly on the Milton Creek, a large area of tidal sea water and marshland that began where our road, Warren Avenue, ended. It was very close to where Hilda lived and Mother was concerned for her safety.

'I do hope, Hilda's alright.'

We later learned that Hilda was unharmed, although she told us later the noise was terrific. Somehow the German bomber pilots had mistaken our creek, with its houseboats, dredging equipment and Asylum buildings for their real target, the Portsmouth Dockyard. Most of their bombs falling harmlessly into the mud.

Under the stairs

Usually the majority of the air raids came at night. As soon as the siren sounded we would quickly take our places under the stairs. Dad said that this was the strongest and safest part of the house. Together with my teddy, tin hat and torch, I would sit in the furthermost recess of the cupboard making myself as small as possible, waiting for the wailing siren to cease and the furore to begin.

First the gunfire, then the deep distinctive throb of the German bombers and the terrifying screams that accompanied their bombs as each one was released over its target. I would sit there, my heart beating wildly; fiercely hugging my teddy bear, waiting for the explosions to follow, praying that we would be kept safe and that the 'all-clear' would quickly sound. When at last we emerged from our place of refuge, we would thankfully make our way up the stairs to the bedrooms.

These unwanted, uninvited night visitors that violated our skies, were not the only ones. Another visitor had actually infiltrated our very own, under the stairs, fortress. It was a grey house mouse who was successfully tracked and attacked with great fervour and eventually caught.

Blitz

The night of January 10th, 1941 would be unforgettable and for ever etched in the city's history. In years to come the people of Portsmouth would still remember that night. 'January the tenth,' they would quietly say. 'The night of the Blitz' [7]

For almost seven hours the German luftwaffe attacked our city. They came, wave after wave, German bombers, showering us with incendiaries and high explosive bombs. And as we huddled under the stairs, now plunged in darkness, Portsmouth burned.

Later we learned whole shopping centres had been set ablaze and many buildings badly damaged or demolished, including churches, hospitals and cinemas, even one of our piers, the Clarence Pier. Overnight our city had changed, landmarks disappeared and over 3,000 people were made homeless, while our

---

[7] This was the first blitz. Official figures confirmed there were 300 planes involved. The number of bombs dropped were a staggering 25,000 incendiaries plus high explosive bombs. There were 2,314 separate fires while 171 people lost their lives with 430 injured. There was a second blitz March 14 - 15 and a third blitz April 27th. Altogether there were 67 separate raids on Portsmouth. Looking back many of these raids now seemed to merge together.

magnificent Guildhall was nothing more than a burnt out shell.

A land mine

After nights of sustained and heavy bombing and, because we were all suffering from various stages of the flu, it was decided that we should sleep downstairs, at least until we had fully recovered.

One night Bert came into the living room looking anxious and agitated.

'I don't like the sound of it,' he said, glancing upwards. 'I feel we should move back under the stairs.'

There had already been some activity that evening with distant gunfire and low flying aircraft, but as yet no warning siren had sounded.

For some reason and without question we followed Bert into the under-stairs cupboard. We had only just taken our places when there was the loudest and most awful explosion I had ever heard. It was as though the whole top of the house had been lifted upwards into the sky and deposited elsewhere leaving us exposed and vulnerable.

I heard Bert say: 'Get ready for the blast.' Suddenly a powerful wave of air swept through the house. It rushed over us, even seeming to go through us, and creating the strangest of sensations, it was followed by the tinkling, almost a musical sound of breaking glass, moving towards us and reaching a crescendo as it levelled with the house and passed beyond it. There followed an eerie silence that was only broken by the belated undulating wail of the sirens.

Shakily we emerged from our hiding place. The front door had blown wide open and many of the glass window panes had been shattered while most of the upstairs ceilings were zigzagged with large ugly cracks but otherwise the house seemed intact.

Bert moved to the open front door and looked outside; we could hear the sounds of ambulances and fire engines already on their way.

'Can you see what's happened?' Mother asked anxiously.

There was a silence and then Bert spoke.

'It's gone,' he said almost in disbelief. 'The end of the road is gone!'

A German land mine (parachute bomb) had been responsible for the destruction and carnage wreaked upon our Avenue that night. The end of the road, houses and shops, were flattened. Only the Public House on the corner, 'The Travellers Joy,' the oldest pub in Portsmouth, remained. No air raid warning had been given.

Life goes on

Bomb sites were everywhere. Houses and other buildings all in various stages of collapse, some reduced to rubble, were all part of an increasingly familiar sight. Whole shopping centres had completely disappeared and some of the big department stores now lay in ruins, their skeletal frames exposed and rusting to the elements for all to see.

Many shop owners vowed that they would open again, some moving to other premises, while at least one large store successfully erected a prefabricated structure within the walls of its original damaged building.

The Airspeed factory where both Dad and Bert worked, although in separate departments, was the first British aircraft factory to be bombed. In all it was attacked on eight occasions.

On one of these raids Bert had flung himself on to the factory floor and as he lay shaking with fear, he had made up his mind that if ever he got out alive, he would leave Portsmouth for ever! Later, strangely enough, this ordeal would have the very opposite effect for, if caught out during a raid, he would continue walking the streets almost without concern for his own safety despite the falling bombs and the flying shrapnel.

During another German sortie[8] two bombs fell on the tool-room area, which was my brother's department, narrowly missing the revolutionary Jig

---

[8] The bomber formation had been heading for Southampton but after being met by six Hurricanes they quickly changed their plans and jettisoned their bombs, two of which landed in the Airspeed tool room area. The department was later moved to Farlington.

borer[9] of which, at that time, there were only three in the country. Fortunately this happened between shifts and there were no casualties.

Despite the raids, the hardships and the heartaches, there flourished a new spirit of community and camaraderie. There were, of course, inconveniences and shortages along with the inevitable queues, but there was also good old Pompey humour and a determination to *see it through!* The city was still "*Alive and kicking!*" People flocked to the "pictures" and other places of entertainment. We avidly listened to the wireless. Some of the BBC announcers became household names – *Stuart Hibberd, Alvar Lidell, Frank Phillips . . . and others.*

We hummed and sang along to '*Music while you work,*' a twice daily programme broadcast directly from the factories to our homes. We laughed at the comedians on '*Workers' Playtime*' and loved *Tommy Handley and his programme ITMA!* And for us children there was one programme we would never miss – '*Children's Hour.*'

I would get as close to our wireless set as I possibly could and would only move away from it when *Uncle Mac* gave the benediction: 'Good night children . . . *everywhere.*'

---

[9] Jig Borers, now commonplace, were at the time revolutionary and operated to an accuracy of a ten-thousandth of an inch. Bert was responsible for the calculations on this machine and later became Chief Jig Borer.

We were determined that the war and the bombing were not going to spoil our fun. We played Cowboys and Indians, Pirates and War games, and we still played football in the streets using our coats as goal posts. And when the bomb sites were cleared or partially cleared, we made them into our adventure playgrounds.

One evening after much persuasion and, with a little help from two of my school friends, Dad[10] reluctantly allowed me to play on the very site where the land mine had fallen.

'Now you just be careful!' Mother cautioned. 'I don't want you getting into trouble.'

I promised and hurried down the road where I joined the other children. We were, all of us, dressed as pirates, with brightly coloured scarves tied around our heads and waists, some wore eye patches, while others carried pistols or brandished wooden cutlasses.

They came from all over the neighbourhood with more and more children joining us, some I had never seen before, it was as though we were part of a strange migration, summoned to converge on this sad, forsaken bomb site, which had suddenly been transformed into a pirates' paradise.

---

[10] My father's reluctance was understandable; on this bomb site many people had lost their lives and homes.

We ran, clambered and climbed; laughed and shouted, fought with each other and "walked the plank." We stayed until dusk, then separating, we melted into the shadows and made our way slowly home.

Ten

The Air Raid Shelter

IN THE BEGINNING OF NINETEEN FORTY-ONE Mr Elliott bowed to the inevitable and agreed we should have our own air raid shelter. When it finally arrived in the July of that same year the shelter's corrugated sections were stacked neatly in a pile at the end of the garden and Bert, using our little box camera, took a photograph of Dad and Mum standing beside it with me balanced high on one of its corrugated curved sheets. Later Bert was able to arrange for two of his friends from church, Alex and Wilfred, to help us with the shelter's preparation and erection.

Alex was a tall Marine stationed in the Barracks at Eastney, not far away. Wilfred was a burly fireman; he was also a conscientious objector. Alex believed passionately that, if the cause was right and just, it was the duty of every able-bodied man to fight for his country. Wilfred believed, equally passionately, that it was wrong under any circumstances to take another life. This of course was the perfect mix to spark off debates, and when these debates became heated, as they sometimes did, Bert would be there to act as a mediator.

On a hot summer's day Alex and Wilfred, happy to forget these differences, agreed to join forces with us. With their shirt sleeves rolled up and grass turfs rolled back, work on the shelter commenced. I watched as they began to dig a large rectangular hole and sometime later a concrete floor was laid. Eventually the corrugated sections were bolted together and Dad made and fixed a massive wooden door to its front entrance.

'That'll keep them out, I wouldn't wonder.' he chuckled.

Finally spadefuls of earth and rocks were thrown or placed over the entire shelter making it a giant rockery.

Our landlord, Mr. Elliot came to inspect our work; sadly he shook his head and departed. His beautiful garden would never be the same again.

A Vivid Memory

'David! Wake up! Wake up!' Mother stands over my bed, gently but firmly, shaking me awake. There is both fear and urgency in her voice.

'David, you must wake up now!' There is no time to put on my dressing gown, instead she pulls the blanket from my bed and wraps it around me.

Suddenly I'm aware of a terrific din from outside. The air raid is already in progress. I make a frantic grab for my teddy bear; to leave him behind is unthinkable. I manage to clutch at his fur and pull him towards me as Mother lifts me from my bed and carries me at great speed downstairs. *(Afterwards Mother will recall that 'fear lent her wings' that night, for she was unable to remember her feet touching the steps!)*

Quickly we make our way through the kitchen, through the conservatory and out through the open door and into the garden. The cold night air stings my face; suddenly I'm wide awake. It is almost as bright as day, the wooden trellis on the garden wall and the rooftops beyond stand out in sharp relief, while above them, searchlights restlessly sweep the sky. Each beam desperately trying to fasten on an enemy raider. Flares are falling. There are bright flashes followed by loud explosions. The noise is deafening. I feel I have awakened into a nightmare. The path that leads to the end of the garden seems to have doubled in length. At last we reach the shelter. Dad holds the door open and helps us inside.

'Where's Bert?' Mother asks anxiously. 'Have you seen Bert?' But my brother is following close behind us. Dad closes the door and at last we are all safely inside.

Often Dad or Bert are out somewhere in the city on fire-watching duty but tonight we are all together.

Mother's hand trembles as she lights the candle. The flame flickers and brightens throwing weird and wavy shadows onto the shelter's corrugated roof and walls. We make ourselves as comfortable as possible on the wooden bunks provided.

'They certainly mean business!' says Dad. 'I don't reckon we'll get much sleep tonight.'

It sounds as though all the guns in Portsmouth are pounding out the sky and still the German bombers come; wave after wave of them, relentless and undeterred. The steady throb, throb of their engines becomes louder and louder.

'They're getting closer.'

Suddenly the bombs are released.

One . . . two . . . three . . . four . . . each one that drops is accompanied by a piercing whistle.

Bert says, *(reassuringly)* 'When you don't hear the whistle you know it's going to be a direct hit.'

I begin to tremble. My teeth are chattering and I can't seem to stop them. Mother wraps the blanket tighter around me and squeezes my hand in hers. Her knuckles are white in the candlelight. She prays quietly.

Now we hear another plane. This one sounds really low. My heart is in my mouth. I'm thinking aloud, my voice comes out very high and wavery:

'Why don't they shoot it down?' I demand, and then

angrily: *'Where are all our Spitfires?'*

The German bomber seems directly overhead. We can hear the deep roar of its engines. Now the bombs hurtle down at us with terrifying screams.

'Please make them miss us!'

We count again.

The last bomb hits the ground with an awful thud and bang! We feel the shelter shudder. Surely it must have landed on our house? At any moment the bricks will come crashing down upon us.

'Phew! That was a jolly close one,' says Dad, and he moves towards the shelter door.

'Dad!' Mother cries out in alarm. '*Whatever* are you doing? Come away from that door!'

But Dad has already opened the door and is peering outside.

'What's happened?' asks Bert. 'Can you see anything?'

'It looks all right.' Dad says at last. 'There doesn't seem to be any damage, not as far as I can tell.'

I'm thinking: *'Please don't let the Germans see our candle.'* Then to our relief he closes the door.

The raid continues, the bombs still fall but they're further away now.

My teeth are still chattering.

One solitary plane is above us. It's a German plane but it sounds as though it's in trouble.

'I think it's been hit!' says Bert. 'I very much doubt

if it will make it across the channel.'

We hear the crippled plane limp away until the sound of its damaged engine is swallowed up by all the other noises. The big guns are still firing, but only half-heartedly. Dad says: 'I think that's it now. It must be nearly all over. Perhaps at last we'll be able to get some sleep.' And as if to confirm it the 'all-clear' sounds.

We stumble from our shelter and look around us. The moon shines down unconcernedly over the houses. By some miracle those around us stand intact and seemingly undamaged. To the left of us the night sky glows an angry red; the searchlights still patrol it and the acrid smell of smoke hangs in the air.

We make our way indoors. Somehow it all seems like an anti-climax.

Mother says: 'I don't think they'll come again tonight. I'm going to make us all a nice hot drink.'

*   *   *

At last I'm back in bed. Mother bends and kisses me. 'You're safe now,' she says and stays beside me. I snuggle down deeper between the blankets with bear beside me and luxuriate in the warmth and the feeling of safety. Soon it will be the morning . . . school . . .

collecting shrapnel . . . meeting friends . . . avoiding enemies . . . playtime . . . I begin to drift . . . Mother quietly tiptoes from the room. 'He's asleep now.' She says. And she goes downstairs.

My trusty tin car in Doods Road Garden

The Anderson air raid shelter yet to be assembled
Warren Avenue Garden

My Mother Hannah Sophia

My Father Albert Ernest (Ern)

With my big sister Renie
Doods Road

Irene Annie (Renie)

Albert Charles (Bert)

Bert in his best Sunday suit

Renie and Wally
on their Wedding day
at St John's Church
Highbury Hill

Renie with baby
Christopher David

My Suffolk Granny

With Granny, my Mother and four of her brothers
David, Joe, Will, Charlie

Brenda with her Mother

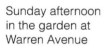
Sunday afternoon
in the garden at
Warren Avenue

Ready for Inspection

Eleven

My Suffolk Granny

IT HAD BEGUN AS AN ORDINARY DAY with a weekly visit to Mother's butcher. As usual there had been a long wait while Mr. Durrant checked each ration book, cut out the coupons, and managed to distribute what little available meat he had to each waiting customer.

He was a dapper, energetic little man, with his neatly clipped moustache and immaculate dress that comprised a straw hat, white coat and blue and white striped apron. He always had a cheery smile especially for my Mother who, I think, must have been one of his favourite customers.

At last we had been served and were on our way home. Mother unlocked the front door and there on the doormat was a letter.

'I wonder who that can be from?' she said, picking it up and studying it anxiously.

The stamped postmark was *Suffolk*.

'It's from your uncle Will,' she said at last. 'I can tell his writing. I hope there's nothin' wrong.'

It was early November; usually Uncle Will's annual letter would arrive just before Christmas. It would be followed by a brown paper parcel, held together (not always securely) with string and sealing wax and inside would be our Christmas dinner – a rabbit!

Mother looked worried and began to open the letter taking it, as she did so, into the kitchen. I put on my slippers and followed her. She was standing by the cooker, her hat still on and the letter in her hand. She was quietly crying.

'It's dear Granny,' she said. 'Your old Granny has passed away.'

This was my Suffolk Granny. I don't remember my other Granny. She had died when I was only three years old and both my Granddads had died before I was born.

To a six-year old the thought of dying was both frightening and depressing. Sometimes on a pre-arranged day and time I would accompany Mother to the telephone box where she would speak to Renie. The nearest phone happened to be beside the cemetery and from over the wall I could see row upon row of graves, many with black and white marble headstones.

'But I don't want you to die.' I had said to my

Mother. 'I don't want you to die, *ever!*'

She had looked at me and smiled. 'We've all got to die someday,' she said gently.

And now Granny was dead.

There must have been many thoughts and memories rushing through mother's head as she began, almost mechanically, to prepare the dinner. Perhaps even recriminations, in fact she said as much.

It was a mistake to be so far away from mother . . . not a good thing.

At heart Mother was still a country girl. She was born and raised in the little Suffolk village of Market Weston where her father had been the tenant farmer of "Fen Farm." She was the only daughter in a large family. Altogether Granny had birthed nine children, two dying in infancy; she was the only girl and because of this she found herself alternately teased or spoilt by her brothers.

Somehow her father and mother had managed to afford her a private education and had sent her to a nearby school in Stanton. It was there she had received tuition in art, music and needlework.

Later she had moved south to the large seaside town of Bournemouth where she had worked as a qualified Governess and Mother's Help to the Beal family who owned a large departmental store there.[11]

---

[11] The store was bombed during the war but later rebuilt. Mrs Beal and Mother continued to keep in touch throughout their lives.

On a visit to her brother, my Uncle Charlie, she had met Dad, fallen in love and together they had started married life in Reigate, Dad's home town. Whenever she could she would visit Granny, and when the children came along, and were old enough, she would take them with her on extended holidays.

Renie and Bert loved these visits, especially Bert who as early as ten years of age would be helping in the fields, loading the beet, and unbeknown to both Mother and Granny, would guide the massive Shire horses from the fields back to the farm. Once my brother had begged Mother for a horse of his own.

'But, Bertie,' Mother had exclaimed. 'If you had a horse, *where* would we keep him?'

His reply had made her chuckle. 'We could always keep him in the lavatory!'

My own memories of Granny and our visits to Suffolk were few and very different for, by now, Granny was an old lady.

Usually we would set off from Reigate stopping off at Kew, the home of my Uncle Charlie and Auntie Ethel, where we would then be taken the rest of the way in Uncle Charlie's motor car. He was one of the few people we knew who actually owned his own car; he also had his own building and decorating business, and made violins as a hobby. I was especially fond of him. He had twinkly eyes, a wonderful sense of humour; loved to tease and had an enormous belly that supported a large nickel watch and chain. I was very envious.

'I want a tummy like yours.' I once told him as we were having tea together. He laughed and shook his head. 'You can't have a tummy like mine.' He said in his sing-song Suffolk voice. 'Why?' he continued. 'Because *(patting his tummy)* this is a business man's tummy. Y'have to be a business man.'

I can recall very little of those long journeys to Market Weston. It is quite likely that I would have slept for much of the way, but I do remember, on more than one occasion, we were startled by pheasants that suddenly flew across our path. One had come directly at us cracking the windscreen and making a terrific bang. The offending bird had finished up in the boot of Uncle Charlie's car and later in Granny's oven.

After motoring through many miles of flat and uneventful countryside, we eventually turned into a narrow lane and out of nowhere there suddenly appeared two small cottages. They both belonged to Granny, and she would be there to welcome us.

To me, Granny looked quite fierce. Her silver-white hair framed a small wrinkled and severe face while her frail bent frame was completely hidden beneath a long black dress.

We followed her into the cottage, it was all very primitive. There was neither gas nor electricity, the rooms were lit with oil lamps, and when water was required it had to be drawn from the well[12] in Granny's garden. I remember standing on tiptoe, peering down into the dark, eerie depths of that mysterious well while Granny slowly cranked the handle sending the bucket disappearing into the blackness below to reappear filled with clear, cold water.

I especially hated the outdoor lavatory, (privy as it was called). I hated everything about it. The large wooden hole you sat on and the terrible carbolic smell that came from the pail beneath it. Most of the holiday I spent in a state of constipation!

The days spent with Granny seemed to pass quite slowly. Once I went with Bert exploring. We made our way through a lane and found ourselves in a tangle of gloomy woodland. I pretended I was an explorer in an impenetrable jungle. Eventually we were forced to turn back when we found the ground boggy and waterlogged and teeming with mosquitoes.

On another day I remember running across to the field directly opposite the cottage and climbing on to a wooden fence; gazing out into the distance. All alone, surrounded only by the smells and sounds of the countryside, I became lost in a world of daydreams, and then, suddenly wishing I were back home in Reigate once more. It was all so different to my brother's and sister's adventures.

---

[12] The old well is still there although now only ornamental.

One day Mother and Dad had wanted to spend a day on their own. I sobbed, threw a tantrum and begged them not to leave me.

'You go on.' Granny told them. 'You go an' enjoy yourselves; he won't be no trouble with me!'

Granny would make certain that this young upstart, this newcomer in the family would know his place. She would stand for no "truck" as she called it, and soon the tears had subsided and I was coaxed back into a good humour. We sat either side of an old table in an outhouse. Earlier I was given some plasticine to play with and soon I was absorbed in modelling while Granny kept a watchful eye on me.

'D'you know somethin'?' she said. 'When you're happy, it make me happy.' Her old face crinkled into a smile, she didn't look a bit fierce now, just kind and gentle.

'Why, it make me as happy as a cricket!'

I laughed.

'D'you know what a cricket is?' she questioned. Of course! I knew all about cricket, my brother had a magnificent sprung cricket bat that Dad had bought for him and that I was not allowed to touch.

Granny shook her head, now it was her turn to laugh. 'Not that sort o' cricket.' And then she explained to me that the cricket she had in mind was a little creature, 'somethin' like a grasshopper.'

'When he's happy,' she continued, 'he make a little

chirpin' noise – like this!' And she began to mimic and I began to model what I thought a cricket might look like. That afternoon Granny and I became friends and when Mother and Dad arrived back at the cottage it was all smiles.

Now Granny was gone. The years of struggle were over. This old country lady had moved on to that *other country* and somehow I knew she was *as 'happy as a cricket.'*

Twelve

A New Arrival

THE TRAIN SLID BETWEEN PLATFORMS and slowed to a halt within feet of the giant buffers that stood at the end of the line. We had arrived at Waterloo station.

From somewhere above our heads the public address system crackled a confirmation. *"London . . . Waterloo! This is Waterloo station . . Will all passengers . . . "*

The remainder of the announcement was lost as carriage doors opened and slammed and passengers poured onto the platform and hurriedly made their way towards the ticket barrier.

I stayed close beside my Mother holding on tightly to the handle of my little leather suitcase, drinking in every sight, sound and smell until we at last passed through the ticket gate and found ourselves in the main station area.

People were moving all around us. Some were

carrying cases; others in uniform had heavy kit bags slung across their shoulders, all heading in different directions. I stood there, hip-high to my Mother, open mouthed, gazing upwards at the enormous blackened glass roof which enveloped the whole building and the criss-crossed iron girders that gave it support and from which pigeons perched and swooped onto the platform below.

Suspended from one of these girders and almost directly overhead was the huge Waterloo station clock with its four faces. Grouped under it were trumpet-like megaphones from which boomed the latest train arrival and departure times together with other information. With each announcement a flurry of passengers and pigeons moved towards their chosen destination. Our destination was Highbury in North London – Lucerne Road; the new home of my sister Renie.

*　　*　　*

Since moving to Portsmouth Mother and Renie had somehow managed to keep up a regular correspondence. Hardly a week would pass without a letter falling on to the mat and Mother excitedly exclaiming: 'It's a letter from Renie.' Eagerly she would pick it up, read it to herself and later when we were all together, read it aloud.

Whenever Renie could she would try and visit us. Sometimes just for the day and at other times staying for a week or longer.

I would always remember my sister as coming and going, When I was just three years old she had worked in Putney as a nanny, once she had taken me with her to play with the children under her care. Later she had moved to work in London. She always had a tale to tell and seemed to generate a sense of excitement. On one such occasion she had some important news for us.

Dad was in the kitchen having his usual nightly strip-down wash, while Mother and Renie sat either side of the fireplace. The glow from the fire lit up my sister's face and brought colour to her pale complexion. Her hair colouring was the same as Mothers but styled with a more modern perm. The dress she wore accentuated her slim figure.

I sat in my little carpet chair directly in front of the fire, dreamily watching the glowing coals and deep in my own imaginary world, content to let the conversation drift across me.

Suddenly Renie moved from her chair. 'There's something I have to show you,' she said and left the room to return a few minutes later with her suitcase. She began to delve into its contents, holding up various items for mother to see; finally she produced a length of cloth patterned in flowers with multi-swirls of colour – blues, greens and purples. It may have been silk. It was the most beautiful material I had ever seen.

'What do you think of it?' she asked.

Mother, for ever the practical one, expertly fingered and felt its texture.

'Whatever made you buy it?' she asked.

'But do you like it?' Renie pressed.

'Yes, it's beautiful, dear, but it must have cost you a pretty packet! Whenever will you wear it?'

Then came the bombshell.

'It's for my wedding dress.' Pause. 'I was hoping you might help me make it.'

I think Mother began to cry.

Renie immediately went over to her and put her arms around her.

'There,' she said comfortingly. 'It's all right, it's all right. Poor old mum, it's been a shock for you, dear.'

It was a shock. It had come completely out of nowhere; Mother seemed quite dazed but gradually recovered her composure and then came the questions:

Who is he?

How long have you known him?

Where did you meet him?

What is his name?

Renie answered the last question first.

'His name is Walter . . . Wally Bray, and you're all going to meet him.' She went on to explain that she had already arranged for her Walter, as she called him, to come down for the weekend, if that was alright, of course. And after more probing she further added that she no longer went by the name of Renie. Wally, she explained, now knew her by her second name *Ann*.

'All my friends in London call me Ann,' she said.

Mother digested this latest information, plied further questions and finally said: 'We'll have to tell your Dad.'

A few days later Wally arrived. He came while Renie was still out shopping and so Mother welcomed him into the house, took his coat and seated him at the living room table.

'Now make yourself at home,' she said. 'You can talk to David while I make us a cup of tea.'

I was sitting in an old wooden orange crate while rocking it to and fro on the floor. Where it had come from I had no idea. It was certainly a long time since it had contained oranges. Now it was a vehicle for my own imagination – a make-believe tank, a ship, an aeroplane or the carriage of a train. On this particular morning it afforded me a little security and a vantage point from which to observe Renie's new fiancé.

Wally was older than Renie, by fourteen years. He was very good looking with dark sleeked hair and appeared to be quite composed, although underneath this demeanour he was probably a little nervous.

He smiled at me. '*Hello, David.*' Wally spoke with a pronounced North London accent and a slight affectation with special emphasis on certain syllables.

'I've heard so much about you!' he said. And then he proceeded to ask the usual questions:

How old was I?
Did I like school?
What did I want to be when I grew up?
Did I like football?

Apparently Wally[13] was a keen sportsman and loved soccer. He had played for two of the top amateur clubs in London, and supported Arsenal. I warmed towards him immediately.

Presently Mother came in with the tea and he asked if he might be allowed to call her '*Mother*'. And later: *Would she mind if he had a cigarette?* As far as I knew no-one had ever smoked in our house before, but from somewhere Mother managed to produce a pewter fish-shaped ashtray and soon both he and Mum were making conversation. That is how Renie found them when she eventually returned home.

Meeting our family for the first time must have been quite an ordeal for Wally but he came through it seemingly unruffled. Bert wrote in his diary later that: *"Renie's young man, Wally, seems quite decent."* When on the Sunday evening Renie and Wally left us for London, and we had waved them goodbye, preparations were

---

[13] In later years Wally involved himself in bowling, becoming president of the Bounds Green Bowling Club, and winner of the coveted Lonsdale Cup.

already underway for a "wartime wedding."

The wedding was to take place in the St. John's Anglian Church[14] on Highbury Hill. Mother and Bert travelled to London to attend the ceremony, while Dad and I remained at home.

One night, later that year, the door bell rang. It was followed by raised excited voices. I was already in bed but I crept downstairs to see what had caused such a commotion. I was spotted.

'What are you doing out of bed?' smiled Mother. She was holding a telegram in her hand, and turning to Dad and Bert she asked: 'Shall we tell him now?' and without waiting for an answer she said: 'Renie's had a little baby, a baby boy!'

'Oh,' I said, and I said it quite nonchalantly as though having a baby boy was an everyday occurrence, which in fact it was.

'His name is *Christopher David.*'

At only seven years of age I had become an uncle.

And now Uncle David and Granny were in London on our way to meet the *New Arrival.* Leaving Waterloo station, Mother followed Renie's instructions and boarded the bus to Southampton Row, changing there for the number nineteen which would take us to Highbury.

---

[14] Now demolished

I think I fell in love with London . . . its tall grey buildings (many now fortified with sandbags, others only partly standing), its yellow brick houses, the red buses and trams, especially the ones with eyes! (an advertisement for "Picture Post") and the black shiny taxi-cabs . . . Its parks, pigeons and people . . . the noise and the bustle and that air of excitement that even the blitz was unable to extinguish . . . I loved it all.

At last we reached Lucerne Road which sloped from the top of Highbury Hill and ended a stone's throw from the famous art deco Arsenal *(the Gunners)* football stadium. Number thirty-one was a corner house and just over half way down the road.

Mother rang the doorbell and we were welcomed inside with hugs and kisses then taken upstairs to Renie and Wally's middle-floor flat. As we followed Renie into the bedroom mother could hardly contain her excitement.

'He's asleep now,' Renie whispered. And as quietly as we could we tiptoed over to the little cot and peered inside.

'This is my tiny Beastie Man!' said Renie proudly.

He lay there quite still beneath the covers, gently breathing, his small pink face just visible, his eyes closed. I think mother found it hard to restrain herself from picking him up and cuddling him there and then. In the next few days we would see and hear much more of Christopher Bray! Mother would have ample opportunity to nurse and busy herself around him despite Wally's gently sardonic admonishment not to *fuss.*

'Don't fuss, Mother!' we would hear him say on more than one occasion. 'Don't fuss, *Mother dear!*' But it made not the slightest difference, Mother fussed all the more. She was in her element and she loved every minute of it.

There was, of course, the usual inquest and the debate that followed:

'Now, who does he look like?' Mother would ask. 'Who does he take after?'

Was he a Jupp?

Or a Bray?

Eventually it was decided he was a little of each but, like many wartime babies, it was thought he most resembled Winston Churchill.

*   *   *

On one morning I asked if I might be allowed out to play. In the street below us a gang of children were noisily and happily playing taking their orders from a tall girl who was obviously their leader. I stood on the kerbside watching them.

'Can I play?' I asked.

'No, you can't play! You don't live 'ere!'

I begged again and again to be allowed to play but each time I was met by a rebuttal or else completely ignored. Feeling rejected and crestfallen I walked slowly along the pavement with my head down. I was desperate to join in the fun. Somehow I had to make them accept me. Already a bold plan was beginning to take shape in my head.

Close to where the children were playing was a brick air raid shelter. Carefully choosing the right moment I came from behind this shelter and pretended to trip, flinging myself on to the roadway in full view of all the children.

'Look 'es 'ad a fall!'

''e's 'urt 'imself!'

Concern for me was spreading.

'Look, 'e's bleedin''

I looked with satisfaction as a small trickle of blood slowly flowed down my bare leg. It was at this point the tall girl took charge. Her maternal instincts aroused she took me under her wing and I was taken home to have my leg bathed and bandaged.

'He's very brave,' she said to the other children and to me she added: 'We'll let you play with us if you want.'

The initiation had been painful. My knee was stinging and thoughts of my self-inflicted wounds brought pangs of guilt.

This, however, was a small price to pay and all was quickly forgotten as I ran up and down that London street with my new friends.[15]

*　　　*　　　*

---

[15] This little episode may well have taken place on another occasion, there were other visits to London but I have included it here.

The week went by quickly; once more we found ourselves standing on a crowded Waterloo station platform. This time Renie was with us carrying her tightly wrapped precious bundle. We had said our "Good-byes" to Wally and were soon on our way to Portsmouth.

When we eventually arrived home, Christopher David was accorded a royal welcome. Renie, now a proud mother placed him in his grandfather's (Grancha's) arms and he was then passed to his other uncle – Uncle Bert. Mother hovered somewhere between them.

That night Bert had seen an advertisement in the local paper of a pram for sale and later went off to procure it. In his diary he wrote:

"Mother brought back Renie with Christopher. Went to Copnor to see about pram. Bought it and I had the pleasure of pushing it back! Fire-watch on top!"

Renie was thrilled with her pram and later Bert penned another delightful snippet in his diary. He wrote: *"Christopher is a sweet little thing and so good."*

Renie's new arrival had quickly established himself in all our hearts. He was now a very special part of our family circle.

Thirteen

Christmas present and past

THE AUTUMN LEAVES had long disappeared, blown away by the four winds or crumpled underfoot. Winter had come, bringing with it the long dark nights and shorter days, but with the promise of Christmastime not far away.

Despite the war with all its uncertainties, separations and shortages, it was still a time for celebration. For as long as I could remember Christmas had always been very special. A magical season, but it was suddenly about to change . . .

When I set off for school that morning I little realized my world was about to collapse! It was nearing home time, we were still busy at our desks making our own Christmas decorations when a boy to the right of me, over the other side of the classroom, suddenly raised his hand.

'Please, miss.'

'Yes, what is it?'

'Please, miss,' he repeated, 'Father Christmas isn't real, is he?' It wasn't really a question, it was a statement.

I couldn't believe what I was hearing. *Not real?*

Another boy put up his hand to speak.

'Yes, miss, there's no such person as Father Christmas.'

No Father Christmas?

'Its only your Dad.'

'Or your mum,' said another boy.

Surely the teacher must say something? Tell them they've got it all wrong!

But when the teacher did speak I was devastated.

'Of course Father Christmas isn't a real person,' she said, 'I'm sure you all knew that.'

I sat there feeling numb. I couldn't wait for the bell to ring.

As soon as I stepped indoors Mother realized that something was wrong.

'What's the matter, dear?' she asked. 'What is it? What's gone wrong?'

I began to explain while tears streamed down my cheeks.

'Oh, David,' she said and repeated my name. 'David, I thought you knew.' and she put her arms around me and tried to console me but it was no use, I was inconsolable.

'But I thought he was real!' and I relived the very first Christmas I could remember, when I was just four years old . . . .

It had been the beginning of a severe winter. Just before Christmas Mother had wrapped me in my warmest overcoat and together we had all braved the snow, to board the crowded little green bus, which bumped and swayed its way to the big Croydon shops.

Some of these shops seemed to have their own Father Christmas. I saw at least two of them, perhaps more. One wore a long red cloak that touched the pavement, the other was clad in a fur trimmed scarlet tunic, breeches and black boots, both with white flowing beards, one surrounded by Christmas trees of all shapes and sizes. But even as I gazed, open mouthed in wonder, I was also reasoning that only one of these could be the *real* Father Christmas.

Leaving the street we entered a large departmental store. I held Mother's hand tightly as the crowds jostled and swirled around us. Suddenly looking upwards I saw what I thought was the best Father Christmas of all.

From a small opening, way above my head and smiling down on me, was the jolliest, roundest face I had ever seen. His eyes twinkled and his long white curly beard flowed over his red-robed body.

Beneath the window of this little booth was a wooden slide, and down this slide came brown paper packages in all shapes and sizes. There was one for each of the children waiting below, and to my surprise I heard my own name being called, and down the slide, gathering pace, had come a parcel especially for me. Surely this *must* be the real Father Christmas?

But now I knew the truth, it was all just make believe. It was at this point that Mother, who was still trying to ease my pain, came up with a truly inspirational idea.

'I know,' she said, 'why don't *you* be Father Christmas?'

Step by step she outlined her plan.

'You'll make a fine Father Christmas.' she enthused and gradually I began to catch her excitement.

A few days later we visited a popular fancy-dress shop, '*U-Need-Us*' quite close to the city centre. This was a child's delight. From floor to ceiling it was stacked with paper hats, face-masks, magic tricks and novelties of every description. We left the shop carrying a Santa mask complete with hood and white beard.

Mother, meanwhile, had hurriedly made me a red tunic and was in no doubt that I would certainly look the part.

And so it was on a cold starlit Christmas eve, I

began my journey that would take me to the house where Hilda lived. My brother who had kindly volunteered to accompany me, lifted me up on to his shoulders and became my trusty reindeer.

When we reached the house I dismounted and we knocked loudly on the front door which was opened almost immediately as if Hilda had been expecting us.

'I've come,' said my brother in his deepest voice, 'I've come to bring you a very important visitor. All the way from the North Pole.'

'I'm very honoured.' Hilda replied as she ushered us inside. 'I'm sure, Father Christmas, you must be very hot in your mask and all those clothes!'

I was not sure whether she or Bert were taking my visit as seriously as they should. Looking sternly through my paper eye-holes I handed Hilda her present. I declined her offer of a drink as that would have meant removing my face mask and I was determined to play the game to the end. After more conversation we wished her a "very happy Christmas," and made our way home.

At last it was time for bed. I looked up at my empty stocking hanging beside me, and found the excitement and expectation that had temporally left me, slowly returning.

Even if there were no *real* Father Christmas perhaps, just for this one special night of the year, his role and mantle would be loaned to all fathers and mothers everywhere. Even I had been Father Christmas for a brief moment and no doubt at some future time I would take on that same role again for my own children. I turned over in bed, took one last look at my stocking, switched off the light and went to sleep.

'Happy Christmas!' Both Mother and Dad were standing by my bedside. They watched as I excitedly plunged my hand into my bulging stocking, unwrapping strangely shaped bundles and covering the blankets with marbles, lead soldiers, white iced mice with long string tails and much more beside.

As I walked down the stairs I was once again greeted with all the wonderful sights, sounds and smells of Christmas. The log fire already alight and warming the house. Carols sounding from the wireless, the dark green Christmas tree fully dressed and sheltering the unopened presents beneath it. And the wonderful smell of Christmas dinner in the making.

Suddenly I realized all the magic, *or nearly all the magic,* was back. After all, Christmas was not about Father Christmas. It was about a little baby. God's own dear Son, leaving heaven to be the Saviour of the world.

Fourteen

The Picture Show

IT WAS ALREADY LATE AFTERNOON and I was slowly making my way home feeling both inward and isolated. None of my friends were to be found. I had trudged the streets, walked around and around the block, through the alleyways and beyond, but everywhere I went seemed deserted.

If there were no street football being played or 'kick the ball trot' there would usually have been someone ready to play marbles up and down the gutters or to flick fag-cards[16] (although both of my collections of marbles and cigarette-cards were now sadly the worse for wear and steadily diminishing.) But today there had been no one to play with. And then with all hope gone

---

[16] Flicking cigarette cards, and cardboard milk tops became a popular pastime. The winner was the one who could flick the furthest and would then take all.

I suddenly heard my name called.

'Juppy!' I spun round. It was a boy I knew from school.

'Are you coming to the picture show?'

'Picture show?'

It was the first I had heard of it.

'In the park.' he continued. 'We're all going.'

'What sort of pictures?' I asked.

'Moving pictures, like in the cinema.'

It sounded exciting! I had never seen a real movie film with talking and music and, as yet I had never been inside a cinema, even though there were at least twenty cinemas in Portsmouth, all only a bus ride away.

Sometimes on a Sunday evening on our way to church we would pass the Plaza, a large cinema at Bradford junction. From the top deck of our trolley bus, looking down from my window, I could see the queue stretching the whole length of the building with more people joining, restless and eager for the doors to open and, for a few moments, I would catch a little of their anticipation and excitement.

Strangely the church building where we worshipped had been one of the first cinemas[17] in

---

[17] Originally known as the 'Grand Kinema' it was one of the oldest cinemas in Portsmouth. Opened in 1911 it was situated in Upper Arundel Street. In 1927 the building was acquired by the Elim Foursquare Pentecostal Church (Now The Oasis Centre) after a crusade visit by George and Stephen Jeffries. The Pentecostal movement was a forerunner to the growing Charismatic movement of today.

Portsmouth to show silent films. It still retained its foyer, the sloping floor and original patterned proscenium. The screen, however, had been replaced with the text: *"Happy is the people whose God is the Lord."*

My friend was speaking again: 'It's going to be good,' he said, 'all about the war, and it's free! Get your mum to take you.'

Suddenly the day had changed. My pace quickened, I couldn't wait to get home.

'Are you *sure* it's in the park?' Mother seemed perplexed when I told her the news.

'I think we'd better make certain.' she said.

Later we discovered that the picture show was not to be held in the park as my friend had supposed but, in the hall belonging to St. James's Church opposite.

When we arrived many of my friends were already there; the hall was almost full but we managed to find seats towards the back. To the front of us and above a small platform was a silver screen and near to where we were sitting was a large projector already loaded with a full reel of film and a second reel beside it. The only other time I had seen a film projector was when I was just three years old. I could still remember it clearly . . .

One morning, very early, my sister, Renie, had taken me with her to Putney where she worked as a childrens' nanny. I had been allowed to stay overnight with her at the big house and to play with the other children.

We had been promised that, if we were very good, we would be allowed to see a picture show. I had almost been excluded, for earlier I had not been very good, and had somehow managed to fall out with one of the children and this had led to tears and my being disgraced. However, as we squeezed onto the settee that evening, all was forgiven.

We sat there expectantly staring up at the white sheet pinned to the lounge wall. Behind us the children's father busied himself with his film projector. After many false starts, flashes and flickers, the improvised screen had suddenly burst into life with a grand procession of, very flat, black and white animated animals.

We had watched, transfixed, as this cartoon carnival of animals paraded before us. There were lions, tigers, elephants, giraffes, zebras and monkeys and many more; one continuous line, each appearing and then disappearing from our view.

Even years later I would see these transient images in reoccurring dreams. The animals, however, would be replaced by a procession of people; some I would recognise. For a brief moment they would pass before me, and then they were gone.

Suddenly the noise in the hall subsided. An official looking man now made his way to the platform and after a few words of introduction the picture show began. One by one the lights were turned off, the projector whirred, the loudspeaker began to crackle and the screen filled with larger than life images all in black and white.

In front of me real people were coming to life, some of them actors, others, animated cartoon characters. I watched, spell-bound. There were films about the army, the navy, and the airforce. We watched firemen, air-raid wardens and auxiliary workers braving the blitz. Other films transported us to the countryside to see the Land Army girls at work on the farms. We entered munition and aircraft factories and met the workers, men and women all playing their part in the war effort.

All these films, of course, had a message. Volunteers were needed! We were encouraged to "Dig for Victory." "Save fuel to make munitions." We were to salvage our waste paper, rags and bones . . . "Make do and mend." And most important to limit our spending and buy "National Savings Certificates."

From time to time a grotesque little creature would pop up on the screen. He had spindly arms and legs with a large belly tattooed with swastikas; this was the *"Squander Bug."* His job was to entice us to spend our money. We were warned to ignore his persuasive whispers! "Don't listen to the *"Squander Bug"* – Buy War Savings!" instead.

Now we were warned to be careful not to give important information to the enemy. We were reminded that *"careless talk costs lives!"* There were spies everywhere! Someone was always listening and it just might be Hitler himself! Now the films began to merge together but there was one that would remain with me . . .

We watched as the pilot adjusted his helmet and climbed into his aeroplane, the propeller spun, the engine roared and the plane took off from the runway. Soon it was flying over enemy territory. Suddenly the pilot glanced from his cockpit window and to his horror discovered the aeroplane had only *one wing!* Sadly there had not been sufficient money for two wings. We watched the plane spiral out of control and disappear from the screen. The answer we were told was simple: More Savings were desperately needed. We were urged to "Buy War Savings!"

"Wings for Victory!"

At last the film show came to an end. We cheered, applauded, and made our way quickly home through the darkness.

'Did you enjoy that?' asked my Mother. I nodded.

'What a lot you'll have to tell your Father.'

I nodded again, still lost in thought while one-winged aeroplanes circled in my head.

Fifteen

The Red Indian

THE SCHOOL TERM was coming to an end and the long summer holidays beckoned. To the casual observer, on that sunny afternoon, I was just another schoolboy hurrying home from school. But that was on the outside, beneath the blue blazer beat the heart of a great warrior, a mighty Red Indian Chieftain.

Over the past weeks our teacher had been sharing with us the story of Hiawatha.

> *"Swift of foot was Hiawatha;*[18]
> *He could shoot an arrow from him,*
> *And run forward with such fleetness,*
> *That the arrow fell behind him!'*

Not only did we learn about Hiawatha, but part of

---

[18] Extract from The song of Hiawatha by Henry Wadsworth Longfellow - 1855

our lesson was to make our own Indian head-dress. We were each given a large piece of stiff paper, pastels and a pair of rounded scissors; in my hand I now held the result of my handiwork, completed that afternoon.

As soon as I arrived home I placed my head-dress firmly in position, and with the fiercest of faces, confronted my Mother with my masterpiece! She seemed suitably impressed. 'Did you make it all yourself?' she asked. I nodded. 'Then you're a very clever boy.'

I looked at myself in the mirror. Who else could I impress I wondered? Someone immediately sprang to mind, it was the little boy who lived next door.

Carroll Wiggins had recently come to stay with his granny, and although he was some years younger, we would often play together. Usually, however, we communicated over the wall and through the open trellis which also acted as a boundary.

Carroll's grandmother, Mrs Wiggins, a friendly soul, was actively involved with spiritualism, as were her family. Once I had been invited into her house to play with Carroll when some of the family arrived. The curtains were drawn, the front room darkened and a meeting convened.

Mother who had heard the sound of voices and singing through the adjoining passage wall realised what was happening, and acutely aware of what might be conjured up in the semi-darkness, hurriedly came to my rescue and escorted me home. For this reason visits beyond the fence were strongly discouraged.

I looked at myself once more in the mirror and made my way into the garden. Carroll Wiggins was nowhere to be seen. I found an old wooden box and placed it upright beside the wall. Carefully I stood on it, raised myself to my full height and peered through the trellis.

Suddenly, without warning, the box went from under me. It happened in a split second. I threw out a hand to save myself and felt a sickening, searing pain in my left wrist. I was in agony. So intense was it that although I wanted to scream out loud no sound would come. When at last a cry did escape my lips it was an awful cry, one that might have awakened the dead! It certainly brought my Mother hurrying from the kitchen; alarm written all over her face.

'Oh!' she cried, 'David, whatever have you done to yourself? Whatever have you done?'

Between great gulps I tried to fill in the details, but the upturned box and the broken flowers told their own story. Mother then did what she could for me. She bathed and bound up my wrist, made up a bed for me on the living room couch and comforted me until the intense pain began to subside a little. We were both relieved when Bert arrived home early from work that evening.

Since moving to Portsmouth my brother had

become a member of the St. John Ambulance Brigade and had recently received his certificate and medallion. Once we had lined the street to wave and cheer as he marched past in procession looking very smart in his black and white uniform.

Now he carefully examined my wrist and from his special white bag produced bandages and a splint and proceeded to place my damaged arm in a large professional looking sling.

'It may be just a very bad sprain,' he said hopefully. 'Anyway, that should make it a little easier.'

But as the evening wore on the pain grew steadily worse. That night I slept fitfully and ran a temperature. In the morning Mother took me to see the doctor.

Doctor Meacle was our family doctor. He hailed from Scotland and mumbled in his own distinctive brogue. A visit to his surgery would invariably conclude with an enquiry as to state of one's bowels.

'Y'need t' keep tha bowels workin'.' he would say. 'Y'need to keep them open.'

On this occasion, however, the bowels were not in question. A quick examination of the wrist and a sudden sharp cry from me was all that was needed.

'I think, mother,' said the doctor, 'I think y'had betta take him ta the hospital. It looks t'me like it's a fracture.'

A visit to the Royal Hospital in Commercial Road and to the x-ray department confirmed the doctor's diagnosis. After the wrist had been set and encased in plaster I was eventually allowed home.

That and subsequent visits to the hospital made a huge impression on me. I had stepped into another world with white coated doctors, ambulance men bringing in their casualties and busy nurses discharging their duties and looking very smart in their starched blue and white uniforms. I especially liked the nurses, they fussed over me and I think I was a little in love with them; not only was I in love with the nurses, *I wanted to be one!* And then the awful realisation hit me, to be a nurse in those days one had to be female. I could never be a proper nurse, for long ago my gender had been decided and it was *irrevocable.* The thought overwhelmed me. I wrestled with it but to no avail.

Once I had been on a shopping errand, and was standing by the counter in the corner Co-op, wearing a coat that came down below my knees and a balaclava pulled tightly over my head, when I was mistaken for a little girl.

'I think this little girl is next!' said the shop assistant. And I left the store, red-faced, humiliated and angry; now I would have almost given anything to have been that little girl who might someday become a nurse and wear a nurse's uniform.

Looking back over this phase in my life, I believe my Mother displayed great wisdom. Not only did she make me a nurse's outfit with apron and hat, but indulged me while I hospitalised my toy soldiers, dressing their wounds, and placing each little lead limb in 'plaster' until finally they were stretchered away, back in their box, ready to fight another day!

Happily these episodes quickly passed and I discarded my nurse's hat, exchanging it once more for the Indian head-dress rejoicing in my own masculinity. I charged up and down the garden. brandishing the beautifully crafted tomahawk my brother had made me; shooting arrows at imaginary Blackfoot and Comanche warriors and sitting cross-legged in my wigwam, smoking the pipe of peace.

With each day that passed my wrist grew stronger and at last the plaster was cut away and replaced by a crepe bandage. Soon after this came a wonderful surprise.

One afternoon Mother called me in from the garden and announced that we were going on a holiday that very afternoon!

'We're off to Redhill,' she told me. 'We're going to stay a few days with your Uncle Frank and Auntie Evelyn,' and added that Dad would be joining us at the end of the week.

I think the reason she had kept the holiday such a well guarded secret was to stop me from getting over-excited. As it was my heart was pounding deep inside my chest as together we made our way to the station.

We boarded the fast train to London changing at

Guildford, and it was while we were waiting on the platform for our connection that I saw my first 'gum chewing' American G.I.

To my Mother's embarrassment I marched over, sat beside him and began to launch at him with questions.

Often on a bus-ride, I would fasten on to someone in uniform and begin a conversation, and although normally shy, I had no trouble communicating. Once I had asked a serviceman if he had ever killed a German.

The man had looked embarrassed. 'I'd rather not answer that question.' he had replied.

My Mother, who had overheard my question and the reply, severely reprimanded me: 'You must never, never ask anyone a question like that again.' She said. It had now been my turn to be embarrassed.

This time my targeted GI was happy to oblige me as I continued to ply him with questions.

'Have you ever seen a Red Indian?' I asked.

'I guess I've seen some.' he drawled.

'What do they look like?' I continued. 'Are they *really* red?'

The American soldier became thoughtful and looked down at his shiny brown shoes.

'Not so much red,' he replied, 'more like the colour of my shoes.'

At this point our train steamed into the station and Mother's relief was obvious. Once again we were off on the last leg of our journey and back in familiar Surrey countryside. In a short while we would arrive at the home of my aunt and uncle.

I remembered Uncle Frank and Auntie Evelyn from my Reigate days; often Uncle Frank would drop in to see us, and every Christmas, he and Aunt Evelyn would throw the most wonderful Boxing Day parties to which we were all invited. They lived in a house they had named 'The Byways', it lay in a dip right on the edge of Redhill common. They had one son, Norman who was the same age as Bert, and a daughter, Audrey.

Audrey was six years older than me. She had big blue eyes, long dark brown plaited hair, an infectious laugh and was great fun to be with and, even though there was that gap in our ages we were still able to play together and enjoy each other's company. In the next few days we became really good friends. Every evening we would run to the common to play and explore it.

We made a little den in a hollow amongst the green and browning bracken, and we clambered up and down the steep tree-clad slopes, slithering, clawing and clinging on to the great twisted tree roots that protruded from beneath the red earth. The white crepe bandage on my wrist was now anything but white!

All too soon, these fleeting, halcyon days slipped away and our holiday finally came to an end. At the end of the week Dad had arrived to spend the last day with us before escorting us back to Portsmouth. I took one more lingering look at the common and countryside that had given so much pleasure, and made my way back to the house. But there was one other surprise in store. Uncle Frank, who, since being at Redhill, I had nominated as my favourite uncle, came into the room carrying a brown paper parcel which he handed to Audrey to give to me.

'You can open it now,' he said.

I unwrapped the parcel and my heart leapt. I could hardly believe my eyes, for inside, neatly folded, was a Red Indian suit complete with tunic, leggings and a head-dress with real feathers!

Uncle Frank smiled at my excitement. 'It used to belong to your cousin Norman,' he said. 'I think he'd have a job to get into it now. We'd like you to have it.'

Back home, resplendent in my newly acquired outfit, I strutted through the garden. Presently I noticed Carroll on the other side of the fence. His eyes were wide with astonishment and envy.

'Where did you get *that*?' he demanded.

I told him.

'You lucky devil!' he said, and he said it again. '*You lucky devil!*'

Sixteen

Sunday Mornings

SUNDAY MORNINGS were the only time the alarm clock remained silent. It was Dad's one chance to have a 'lay-in'. Unfortunately the neighbourhood cockerel was unaware of this and felt it duty bound to throw back his head and awaken the dawn.

'Blooming cockerel!' Dad had even written to the editor of the *Portsmouth Evening News* vehemently expressing the opinion that the rooster's anti-social behaviour had far out-weighed its wartime usefulness. It was all to no avail.

'Blooming cockerel, I'd like to wring its neck!' And I believe he would have.

Meanwhile, quite unconcerned, the rooster continued his raucous crowing; he was joined by another of Dad's pet aversions – a neighbour's dog who was determined to have his say and to say it even louder. His harsh persistent bark reverberated and echoed across the alleyways.

'Jolly dog!' Dad had written another letter, in it he suggested that if anybody *had* to have a dog then they might, at least, have the decency to look after it properly and keep the creature quiet. Again this letter was received with little sympathy by editor and public alike.

Eventually the duo quietened; Dad dozed and after a few minutes Mother would make her way downstairs to put on the kettle for a cup of tea and prepare the breakfast. This was my cue to creep out of bed and climb into Dad's big double bed. I would snuggle down beneath the warm sheets and wait until I sensed my Father begin to stir.

'Dad,' I began tentatively. 'Dad! Are you awake?'

His little *'mosquito'* as he sometime called me was about to end his rest.

My Father gave what sounded like a grunt.

'Tell me a story.' Another grunt followed.

'Please tell me a story.' In a sleepy voice Dad would begin:

> *Dark was the night and stormy,*
> > *The Brigand chief stood on the shore.*
> *'Tell us a tale,' said he to Bill.*
> > *And Bill began as follows:*
> *'Dark was the night and stormy . . .*

'No! Not that story,' I interrupted. 'A *proper* story.'

Our old Gaffer's a very nice man.
He tries to teach us all he can.
Reading, writing and arithmetic,
And he don't forget to give us the stick!
When he does he makes us dance,
Out of England into France,
Out of France into Spain;
Over the hills and back again.

Dad loved these little monologues, he had a string of them and had I not interrupted him, he would have continued them all morning or at least until it was time to get up.

'Tell me a *Tommy and Nora* story,' I pleaded.

Tommy and Nora were Dad's very own creation. They were brother and sister who had incredible escapades with pirates and brigands yet somehow managing to escape from the hands of their wicked captors ready for their next adventure. I loved these stories and I loved these early Sunday mornings when I had Dad all to myself and felt a special closeness to him.

My father was a remarkable man. At a young age he had set his heart on becoming a draughtsman. He certainly had the ability and gifting, but it would have meant going to college. When money and other circumstances would not allow for this he decided instead to serve his time as an apprenticed carpenter and joiner.[19] A trade in which he excelled.

Much of Dad's working life had meant travelling and being away from home; often staying in lodgings. He had worked on numerous projects in various locations, among them the construction of the Quaker Model Village at Jordan's in Uxbridge. He had built boats on the river Thames at Chertsey; and had been involved in the construction of Welwyn Garden City,[20] London's first satellite town. It was here that Mother and baby Renie joined him to set up home, and while they were there, Bert was born.

On the surface, Dad sometimes appeared to be austere, strict and something of a disciplinarian but, like so many people, he had his contradictions. He could be kind, caring and compassionate.

He was not a demonstrative man; never easy to know. I think he found it difficult to show his true feelings or affections. Dad despised sentimentality, 'slushiness' as he called it, yet he dearly loved Mother and deep down he was a romantic. He loved reading, especially poetry, and often he would read aloud from the leather-bound Longfellow book of poems that Mother had given him one Christmas. He also loved music, particularly the classics and the great hymns of the church. As a boy he had sung with his father in the

---

[19] This was the same firm as Grandfather had worked for as a painter and decorator. He was a skilled tradesman much sought after by the local gentry.
[20] This was in 1922.

St Mark's Church choir, and had been taught to play the piano by the celebrated organist of St. Paul's Cathedral.

Sometimes he would be asked to play the piano or organ at the local church, but he would never push himself forward, in many ways he was self-effacing yet he was never frightened to speak his mind, often with devastating effect! He hated injustice and would be quick to champion a deserving cause.

Dad had a serious nature yet he was not without a sense of humour and he would often chuckle to himself or even roar with laughter if a joke appealed to him. He had no time for anything 'smutty' but on the other hand he was no prude. 'To the pure all things are pure.' he would say. As a young man he had been fond of the music hall and it was Dad who would take me to see my first pantomime. Once he told me how he had taken his own father to Brighton to see the farce *Charlie's Aunt.*

'We laughed so much we thought our sides would split!'

The significance of this was that my Grandfather had been able to laugh for the first time since the death of William,[21] his favourite son, who had died from a fever while serving in Mesopotamia. It always gave

---

[21] L/Cpl William Henry Jupp served in the Queen's Royal West Surrey Regiment. He died in Mesopotamia at the age of 22 from a fever. During his time in service he and my Father engaged in correspondence. Copies of his letters, together with short autobiographies can be seen at the Imperial War Museum in London, also in the Reigate Museum in Priory Park.

Dad great pleasure to relate this episode.

Father was a humble man, he had a simple faith and a Bible verse he often quoted might well help to sum up his life:

'He hath showed thee, O man, what is good; and what doth the Lord require of thee, but to do justly, and to love mercy, and to walk humbly with thy God.' Micah 6:8

Sometimes on a Sunday morning I would persuade Dad to tell me stories of when he was young.

'You don't want to hear about that – when I was a boy.' he would protest, but after a little more prompting a smile would cross his face and he would begin to relive those long ago days when life had been so different.

He would tell me some of the mischievous pranks that he and his friends had got up to. How they had tied string to letter boxes, knocking and running away to watch from a distance as the first front door opened setting off a chain reaction down the street. 'You should have seen all those faces!' he chuckled at the thought of it. We were just skylarking,' he would say.

Then he would go on to tell of some of the other tricks they had got up to and how he and the lads had roamed the Reigate hills, searching for and catching adders, and exploring the countryside.

On one occasion, a Bank Holiday, Dad and his very good friend Pearce Barnard, who often featured in his stories, had decided to walk to London. They had set off early in the morning and made their way across the Surrey hills until after many miles of walking they had at last reached the city. They then did some sightseeing and eventually ended up at the Monument and decided, unwisely, to complete their day by climbing right to the top.[22] They arrived back home late that night completely exhausted.

'We were absolutely *jiggered,*' Dad confessed. In fact it took him over three weeks to get over this punishing escapade.

'Tell me another story,' I begged. 'Tell me the story of how you were nearly caught by the baker!'

'Well now,' Dad would begin. 'It all happened late one evening just as it was getting dark. We were on our way home when one of the lads picked up a stone and threw it. It landed smack on the baker's posh cart!'

It appeared that this act of vandalism had been quite accidental but unfortunately the lad's idle throw had missed its target and had made a large crack on one of the side panels of the highly polished delivery cart. The baker had been absolutely furious.

'He charged at us like some demented animal!'

'I'll have you for this!' he roared. 'I'll get you, you see if I don't.'

All the boys had scattered except my Dad.

'Run, Ernie!' they shouted. *'Run!'*

---

[22] 319 narrow winding steps

The only avenue of escape lay in the grounds of a big house – the *Toff's* house, as my Dad called it, belonging to one of Reigate's gentry. Quick as a flash Dad managed to open the iron gates, squeeze through them and had then disappeared into the garden, hoping to give the baker the slip. Meanwhile the baker, hot in pursuit, and bellowing out threats had knocked at the door of the house and had managed to enlist the help of the servants.

'My heart was beating so fast,' said Dad. 'It was fit to burst.'

Dad, now quite breathless, ran deeper into the grounds, as he did so he could hear the voices of the servants getting louder and louder and could see their lanterns swinging and illuminating all that lay before them.

'He won't get very far, there's a high wall at the end of the garden; he'll never climb over that!'

By now Dad was becoming very frightened.

'We'll soon put a stop to his game!'

Suddenly Dad turned and found himself facing an impossibly high and seemingly unscalable wall. It would be only a matter of time before the game was up.

'Tell me how you escaped?' I asked, but I already knew the answer for I had heard the story many times before.

'I took one look at that wall, heard the sound of those men

out for my blood and miraculously fear lent me wings.'

How Dad had managed to hoist himself over that wall to freedom he would never know, but somehow he had! He left behind some mystified and empty handed servants and a very enraged baker, to once again rejoin his friends.

'Tell me . . .' I began, but now I could hear the clink of cups. Mother was coming up the stairs bringing a tray with the tea.

'You're not telling him those naughty things again what you got up to?' But she was smiling. 'Have your cup of tea now. Breakfast will be ready soon.' And we could smell the bacon.

Suddenly the mood changed. It was back to the present. It was time to get washed and dressed, have breakfast, put on the polished shoes that Dad had brushed and buffed the night before. Then it was out the front door, through the park, on to the trolley bus and into church.

This was my Sunday morning.

Seventeen

The Living Room Table

WE CALLED IT THE LIVING ROOM TABLE because that is where it lived. It was just a simple, dark stained wooden table that Dad had made some years earlier. And yet for all its simplicity of design it had been made beautifully, for Dad was a perfectionist. As far as I was concerned it had always been there, an everyday part of our lives. It was with us at Doods Road, and it preceded us to Portsmouth where it dominated a large proportion of the living room at Warren Avenue.

Sometimes Mother would complain: 'It's too big,' she would say. 'It takes up far too much room, perhaps we ought to get rid of it.' But like everything Dad made, it was made to last, and it was destined to remain. The table was a symbol of continuity, an endearing part of the fabric of our life together until Dad finally retired and we were then forced to move to smaller accommodation.

Of course, it was not the only table we gathered round. There was the kitchen table. This was pushed up hard against one wall bearing an assortment of tins and other packages permanently grouped together.

In the far corner stood the 'Weetabix' tin that housed my 'Sunnybisks', and alongside it, a bright red oblong tin that contained cream crackers; the gold embossed printing on the side reminding us that: *'East, West, Home's Best.'* And beside it, the 'Shredded Wheat' Box, with its famous slogan: *'Britons make it, it makes Britons.'* This was Dad's favourite morning cereal and close to it was the distinctive bottle of 'Camp' coffee, and a jar of 'Horlicks.' There was also a small black leather covered book, a dog-eared copy of *'Daily Light,'*[23] containing a selection of scripture verses that Dad would read aloud each morning and evening.

This was the table where we ate most of our meals. It was also where Mother prepared, mixed and made her fruit cake and buns, ready for Sunday tea to be served at our other table, a pretty little round gate-leg table that stood in the front sitting room. This would be dressed with a clean laundered table cloth and laid up with Mother's best rosebud bone china tea service. These two tables hold many memories and both played a special part in our everyday life, yet it is the

---

[23] Published by Samuel Bagster & Sons Ltd

living room table that I remember most of all.

One of my earliest memories must have been when I was just three years old. It was nearing my bedtime, the family stood around the table discussing some topic or other seemingly oblivious of me. I was hiding beneath the table and about to discover just how solidly my Father had made it. Suddenly standing to my feet, my head made sharp contact with its underside; there was a terrific bang.

'Oh, my giddy aunt!' cried Mother, *(a favourite expression)* 'Whatever was that?' And stooping down she gathered me up and smothered me to her aproned bosom.

'There, there . . .' she soothed and rubbed my aching head.

My sister Renie spoke: 'What was he doing under there? That's what I'd like to know.'

For some reason I didn't cry. 'You'll have a nasty bruise there.' Mother said and added: 'You're a very brave little boy.' and turning to the others, 'Isn't he brave?'

'Naughty table!' said my sister.

Somehow I knew the table was not to blame. The pain had been self-inflicted. I must bear the punishment.

It was to this table we had anxiously gathered on that fateful day in September, pressing against its sides and straining to hear the latest news from the little crackling, whistling wireless set; learning we were at war with Germany. I had slid quietly away leaving the 'grownups' to ponder and discuss the implications of that war and some of the changes that would need to be made in the near future.

A few days later there were two new faces at our living room table. They belonged to a brother and sister, the two evacuees we had been asked to billet. In the years that followed they would be joined by many faces both new and old.

There were aunts, uncles and cousins, friends and family; people we knew from church – an exuberant Pastor Coleman who was very dear to all of us. One morning when he called in to see my parents, I was on the floor in the corner of the room with my brick-box open, engrossed in building, but even as I lay there I was aware that the conversation around the table was more serious than usual.

My Mother's voice broke my concentration. She called me over motioning me to sit on the couch.

'Pastor Coleman has something important to say to you'.

I sat down and faced him and learned that he was sadly leaving us and moving to another church. I'm not sure I fully understood all what was being said, but I knew we would all miss him.

Pastor Coleman spoke again. 'David,' he said. 'Before I go I want to teach you a little song.' And he began to sing and with his hands to do the actions:

'Zacchaeus was a very little man,
A very little man was he.
He climbed up into a sycamore tree
For the Saviour he wanted to see.
And when the Saviour passed that way
He looked up to the tree . . .'

At this point his voice had boomed out across our tiny living room, and with one stubby finger, pointing at the ceiling he echoed the command of Jesus:

'ZACCHAEUS! COME DOWN!
I'm coming to your house for tea . . .'

Then there was the solemn faced Mr. Elliot, our landlord who, over a cup or two of tea, would try to make sense of an 'upside-down' world, while mother patiently listened but also managed to say her piece.

And it was at this same table that Wally, Renie's young man first introduced himself and discussed with Mother plans for an early wedding.

During the war years we were joined by members of His Majesty's Forces and the Auxiliary Services: representatives from the Army, Navy and Royal Marines, and even two Land Army girls who were far from home. Dad had discovered them one Sunday evening waiting forlornly at a bus stop and had promptly invited them home for supper.

However it was usually at Sunday lunch that Mother and Dad entertained.

Dad would sit at his accustomed position at the head of the table, would carve the meat and say grace. Sometimes we would sing it together:

> *'Be present at our table Lord,*
> *Be here and everywhere adored.*
> *These creatures bless, and grant that we*
> *May feast in Paradise with Thee.* – Amen.'

It was at one of these dinners that we met Bert's future wife, Muriel who was serving in the Auxiliary Fire Service. I listened with open mouth as she shared with us the chilling story of a ghostly presence in a house where she and the other girls were billeted.

Across the years the hum of conversation reverberated – animated, trivial and sometimes profound. There were debates, arguments, and on many occasions the old table was rocked with laughter. There were also times when tears fell and stained its surface.

On each birthday we would gather to sing and blow out candles. And we would all celebrate Christmas, eagerly dissecting and devouring Uncle Will's Suffolk rabbit. All, that is, except for me. The sight of that little furry creature hanging by his ears in mother's larder, waiting to be skinned, did little to excite my appetite.

But it was not only a place where we came together to eat, it was also somewhere we could work and play. Out would come the ludo, the snakes and ladders, dominoes and draughts. Draughts were Mother's favourite game, and she insisted on *'huffing.'* How often we would hear her say: 'If you don't take me I shall have to *'huff'* you! And she did with great relish.

We played table-tennis and 'blow football.' We blew with all our might until our cheeks ached and we turned giddy, determined to see that little ball bounce in the back of the goal net. Later 'blow football' would be superseded by the more sophisticated *'Subbuteo.'*[24] Sometimes the table top was a parade ground for my lead soldiers or a rolling prairie with cowboys and Indians and paper wigwams. It became a zoo and a travelling circus and much more.

At other times I would sit beside it, reluctantly, struggling with my homework. Dad would write letters, sort out accounts and draw up plans. Bert would sketch and paint, already showing early promise as the accomplished artist he would some day become.[25]

---

[24] Table Soccer invented by P. A. Adolph. Not available until after the war.
[25] Bert's collection of 'Portsmouth Prints' have been sold and shown in many countries across the world.

And for Mother, who was a skilful dressmaker, it became her work table. We would watch as she pinned her paper patterns on to the cloth, carefully cutting each segment of the garment and finally sewing them together on her clattering 'Singer' sewing machine.

On one unforgettable occasion the living room table became an operating table. For some reason my baby teeth wouldn't budge, they refused to make way for the new teeth and tenaciously remained rooted to my jaws. The solution was to have them forcibly removed. After consultations with the dentist it was decided to perform this operation at home. Doctor Meacle would be there to administer ether and the dentist would make the extractions while I was lying on the specially prepared table, directly under the bright overhead light.

That evening, at the appointed hour, both the dentist and doctor arrived. Their bags were opened and their instruments placed with precision on the table. It was at this moment that my courage failed me and I fled for refuge to the lavatory bolting the door behind me! The minutes ticked by. Mother pleaded with me, my brother reasoned and my Father threatened.

'If you don't come out there soon the dentist is going home.'

That seemed like good news to me.

'I'll give you just *three* to open that door!'

I was under siege.

'Now try to be brave. It will soon be over and you'll be glad you've had it done.'

And so I bowed to the inevitable and surrendered myself to my 'executioners.'

Under the ether I found myself drifting into a brilliantly coloured 'nursery-rhyme' land. I began, with Jack and Jill, to climb the hill and each time we reached the top I would feel, through the haze of the anaesthetic, a searing, drawing pain that only subsided as we made our descent down the hill only to return as we once again ascended it. In all, this was repeated eight times. Finally I awoke in tears with a bloody mouth feeling wretched and exhausted. I was calmed by my brother and later by my Father reading to me the tale of the much loved Hiawatha.

During the early part of the war our table had yet another role to play. Before the Anderson shelter had been installed the two safest places indoors were under the stairs and under the table. When the night bombing raids became heavy and persistent Mother would make up a bed for us on the floor and we would actually sleep beneath it.

This also happened during times of sickness when we were too ill to brave the cold and damp of the night air. Had one of Hitler's bombs targeted our house it is doubtful we would have survived but under Dad's table we felt a certain security and sense of wellbeing to which we were very grateful.

As I write this, I'm wondering what became of Dad's living room table. Does it still exist? Is it in a state of disrepair – in some garden shed or garage? Or is it still in service – perhaps with a few more knocks and bearing new scars, but all these only adding to a richer and ever growing patina?

I would like to think so.

Eighteen

Sickness

WHEN SICKNESS CAME AS IT OFTEN DID, Doctor Meacle would be there to combat it. He would arrive with his brown leather bag, and armed with stethoscope and thermometer; he would examine, diagnose and prescribe treatment.

A particularly virulent and repetitive illness was influenza – the dreaded flu.

Dad was especially vulnerable to it and when he caught flu it was always serious. He would run a very high temperature, sometimes making him delirious and it would be a battle to bring the temperature down and so save him from pneumonia. When an outbreak of flu came it was almost certain that more than one member of the family would fall victim to it so keeping the good doctor busy.

On at least two occasions Renie was struck down

with sickness. During one of her visits with Christopher, she had suffered a severe attack of bronchitis, and on a further visit she developed something far more serious. It was towards evening when she first complained of stomach pains. These pains grew steadily worse and became severe, lasting throughout the night and followed by violent sickness. In the morning Mother sent for the doctor.

'Well, m'dear,' said Doctor Meacle in his familiar Scottish manner. 'I think we'll be sending you to the hospital.'

But Renie refused to go. 'I'm not going to the hospital!' she said. 'There's no way I'm going to the hospital.' And although the doctor remonstrated with her, she was adamant.

Doctor Meacle shook his head and made for the door. 'If she won't go to hospital,' he said turning to my Mother, 'then I'll have t' wash my hands of her.'

He looked weary; he had never really got over the sudden death of his practice partner, Doctor Williams, yet he had carried on in his own uncharismatic way, a man of few words; solid, caring and conscientious.

'Let me know as soon as she changes her mind,' were his parting words.

I watched helplessly as Renie lay on the floor clutching her stomach. Her dressing gown was partly open revealing her thin white legs that were patterned with blotchy red circles as a result of being too close to the fire.

Mother came back into the room. 'It's no good Renie, dear; you know you can't go on like this. You must do as the doctor says. You *must* go to hospital.'

'But it will go.' She said. 'I've had this pain before – it will go.'

But it didn't go and at last the pain and common-sense prevailed. By lunchtime the ambulance arrived and Renie was on her way to the hospital. And only just in time, the doctor's diagnosis of acute appendicitis had been correct, only now it had turned into life threatening peritonitis. It had been 'touch and go' and would take several weeks before she fully recovered.

I too had my share of sicknesses. There were the usual childhood illnesses, chicken-pox measles, and of course, the colds and flu, plus a mysterious allergy that was later diagnosed as *acidosis* and had meant placing me on a special diet.

The best part of being ill I had discovered (if there was a best part) was that moment when the fever leaves one and I was able to sit up in bed and begin to take notice. I had just reached that point now.

For a long time, it seemed, I had been running a high temperature, burning up or shivering with my head pounding. On several occasions our regular doctor had come to examine me and to prescribe his usual panacea: 'Make sure, M'ther, he drinks plenty of water and t'keep those bowels open.'

And then at last, with the temperature subsiding, here I was propped up with pillows on the living room couch in a specially improvised bed mother had made for me.

My bear sat beside me and surrounding us and almost covering my eiderdown was a great pile of Rupert books.

Mother came into the room. 'Now what can we give you to eat?' she asked. 'You have to get your strength back. Is there anything you fancy?' And she began to coax my appetite with a list of my favourite foods, but I already knew what I wanted.

As soon as mother left the room I reached out for one of the Rupert books that John, a friend from church, had been kind enough to lend me. These were books which ranged from early editions to present day annuals. I eagerly read and re-read them. My favourite story was the one where Rupert joins the circus.

One Sunday afternoon, before the war commenced, and while we were still living in Reigate, Dad and Mother had taken me on a walk. All had seemed quite uneventful until suddenly we were startled by the clip-clop, clip-clop of horse's hooves, the jangle of harness and the rumble of wheels.

'David!' cried Mother. 'Quickly! Look! Circus caravans!'

From out of nowhere, two horse drawn caravans had appeared and had swiftly careered past us, swaying as they went.

In the second caravan had been a white faced clown, smiling and waving. It was all over in moments, and yet the memory of that clown with his painted face, sequinned hat and tunic would remain with me forever.

All this and subsequent stories had helped to birth and fuel an appetite for the world of the circus, a world that the long war years had denied me. Perhaps now that the war was nearly over I would get to see my very first real circus.

Presently Mother came back into the room, she was carrying a tray with a plate of steaming hot mash and extra thin 'soldier boys' with an even thinner coating of margarine and Marmite.

'There, eat this up,'. 'It will do you good.'

It didn't taste quite the same as I had expected but I managed to eat it all and could almost have asked for more.

Later, one afternoon, Mother came and sat with me. The *'Cossor'* wireless set that stood in the corner of our living room was already switched on and together we listened to the music. So many times, both in sickness and health, I had laid or sat on that faded old couch, listening to the friendly wireless with its host of familiar voices and ever changing programmes of music, entertainment and information and, of course, the news bulletins that helped keep us in touch with the latest war developments.

These had not always been good. There were, in

those early days, terrible setbacks and uncertainties; the sinking of British ships; reports coming through of the evacuation of Dunkirk; the 'Battle of Britain;' the nightmarish prospect of a German invasion, then the Blitz. All that had changed. It was now early May, nineteen forty-five. Hitler was dead, the confirmation we had been waiting for had officially been given. Our British and Allied troops were advancing deep into the enemy lines. Many villages, towns and cities were surrendering and an announcement might be made at any moment to the effect that the war in Europe was at an end.

Suddenly our listening was interrupted by a loud knocking at the door.

'Now I wonder who that can be?' Mother got up and made her way along the passage. Presently she returned to fetch her purse.

'Who is it?' I asked.

'I'll tell you in a minute. It's a surprise!'

I strained my ears to listen but without success. At last Mother closed the front door and came back into the room. She was holding a piece of paper.

You are invited to a VICTORY PARTY, it read, and on it was my name.

Some of the ladies in the neighbourhood had met together and were organising a street party which would take place as soon as peace was declared.

'So now, David, you really will have to get well –

quickly.'

'I'll try.' I said. 'I really will try.'

I really did want to go to the party and secretly I hoped the war wouldn't end, *not just yet*.

Nineteen

Street Party

DURING THE WAR YEARS Bert kept a diary, not that he recorded many of the events of those years, but on the 8th of May 1945 he had written in very large capital letters:

VE DAY   VE DAY   VE DAY   VE DAY
National Holiday. Great rejoicing. Thanksgiving. PM officially announces to nation the end of hostilities at 3pm.

On every street flags were flying and houses decorated. From under our own top front bay window Dad had hung an enormous Union Jack which fluttered proudly in the light breeze. It was in pristine condition and had been kept in one of the bedroom drawers waiting for this day. Probably the last time it was used was to celebrate the Coronation of King

George VI and Queen Elizabeth and before that the 1914–18 Armistice of the First World War.

Down in the street below preparations were being made for the Victory Party. The end of the war hadn't waited for me to get better! I was still unwell and feeling very weak. I sat in a chair by the window wearing a jumper over my pyjamas, wrapped in a warm dressing gown and looking down, through two layers of net curtains, at the street below. For some bizarre reason I didn't want any of my school friends to see me. I was almost paranoid about this. From my vantage point I watched as trestle tables were assembled and covered with table cloths followed by chairs brought out from various houses, and placed alongside them.

Now that the war with Germany had finally come to an end there was almost a sense of anti-climax; an unreality about it. In some ways it was as if the war had been over for a long time. The last night air raid on Portsmouth had been a year before; one month later, on June the sixth, D-Day, a great armada of ships and planes set off from our shores and the long awaited invasion had begun. Shortly afterwards, Hitler, sensing defeat had launched his secret weapon – the V1 rocket or 'doodlebug' as we called it. These had mainly been targeted on London although two managed to find their way to Portsmouth. The first had landed in Locksway Road not very far from my school the second one in Newcomen Road, Stamshaw.

I had watched, from the garden, this squat pilot-less plane making its unimpeded and sinister way over to the northwest of the city, belching fire from its rear and making that strange buzzing sound that earned it its other name – 'the buzz bomb.' Moments after it had passed overhead its engine had suddenly died. Then came that strange and terrible silence as it fell from the sky followed by a dull thud. Later we learned there had been fifteen deaths that day and eighty-two casualties.

The V1 had been followed by the more deadly V2 rocket. Once again these had been targeted on London, and it was at this time Renie and baby Christopher were evacuated to Wales and then later to Portsmouth. It was while Renie had been staying with us that she had suddenly been struck down with appendicitis. Christopher was now eighteen months old, no longer the sweet sleepy little baby, but now completely mobile and greatly into demolition! They stayed with us until the rocket sites had been dealt with and the danger past.

The only other intrusion over our city had been a German reconnaissance plane. From either side of our garden fences, Caroll Wiggins and I had watched it flying overhead at an incredible height, sharply illuminated in the late evening sunlight. The sirens had remained silent but the AA guns kept up a constant barrage, although most of the shells seemed to have burst well short of their target. And then, suddenly the plane had lost height, it had started to dive, falling from the sky with smoke and vapour streaming from its tail.[26] A shout went up from the adjoining gardens:

'It's been hit! It's been hit!' Cheering and clapping followed.

Carroll and I watched it spiral out of sight behind the houses followed by two white billowing parachutes drifting slowly downwards until they had disappeared from our view. We later learned that the aircraft and its crew ended up in the sea; the parachutists were eventually rescued. This was the last German plane we were to see.

Outside preparations for the party were almost complete. Mother came into the room and stood behind me looking out of the window.

'Are you sure you're warm enough?'

I nodded.

'It won't be long now I shouldn't think,' she continued. 'What a shame you're going to miss it all.'

Even as she spoke the street began filling with children. It was as though the magical Pied Piper had suddenly materialised and was piping his irresistible

---

[26] It was later revealed an ATS Servicewoman had been responsible for this 'predictive' remarkable shooting.

call. Out of the houses they came, boys and girls in all shapes and sizes, some wearing paper hats and waving flags, laughing and shouting, all making their way to the trestle tables where an army of pinafored ladies and other helpers waited to serve them. There were jugs of lemonade, assorted sandwiches, jelly and ice-cream and home made cakes.

'Look.' cried Mother. 'Do you see the clown?'

Sure enough a clown with a shock of red hair and even redder nose was making his way around the tables, no doubt telling jokes, certainly making the children laugh. I suspected he wasn't a real clown, probably one of the neighbours dressed up, but the children loved him. There was also a juggler who threw balls up above his head and sometimes caught them.

By now my inhibitions were fast disappearing, I moved closer to the window and as I did so I was seen by some of my school friends. They must have caught sight of my pale and pasty face looking through the net curtains and they waved at me. Richard, one of our school 'gang leaders,' *(I was never quite sure whether I was in his gang or out of it.)* saw me and mouthed: Was I feeling better? And was I coming down to join the party? And would I be coming back to school?

I shook my head and he actually looked sympathetic and then disappeared mingling with all the other children until I lost sight of him.

As we watched, the doorbell rang. Mother went to answer it returning moments later with a bowl of ice-cream and a small piece of iced victory cake. Slowly I began to eat keeping my eyes fixed on the street below.

Once the tables were cleared the children began to play games, finishing up with a loud sing-song. And then it was all over. One by one they were rounded up by their parents while some of the older children slowly drifted away until soon the street was almost deserted. I got back into bed and lay there; I must have dozed for when I opened my eyes it was already starting to get dark. It was now the turn of the 'grown-ups.'

Almost directly in front of our house and in the middle of the road a huge bonfire had been built. It was already alight and neighbours were still bringing out pieces of wood and old furniture and adding these to it. As the flames took hold it began to crackle and spit sending sparks and smoke upwards into the darkening evening sky. Meanwhile more people began to gather. Someone with a piano accordion began to play, and Richard's father, wearing black football referee's shorts and carrying an improvised baton began to take charge conducting the singing and leading the dancing.

I watched from my window as the 'grown-ups' snaked and swayed their way around the brightening bonfire. The strains of familiar war and other songs echoed throughout the street.

Roll out the barrel, we'll have a barrel of fun.
   Roll out the barrel, we've got the blues on the run.
Zing boom tararrel, ring out a song of good cheer.
   Now's the time to roll the barrel,
For the gang's all here . . .

And on and on it went . . .

She'll be coming round the mountain when she comes.
   She'll be coming round the mountain when she comes
She'll be coming round the mountain,
   Coming round the mountain,
Coming round the mountain when she comes.

The singing became louder and the dancing more uninhibited.

She'll be wearing pink pyjamas when she comes,
   She'll be wearing pink pyjamas when she comes,
She'll be wearing pink pyjamas, wearing pink pyjamas,
   Wearing pink pyjamas when she comes . . .

I began to feel very sleepy and turned away from the window; Mother came into the room, closed the curtains and helped me climb into bed, then she tucked me up, kissed me *Good-night* and left the room.

Outside the fire still burned brightly its flames lighting and warming my bedroom, while outside the 'grown-ups' were still singing:

> *'It's a lovely day tomorrow,*
> *Tomorrow is a lovely day . . .'*

In the days that lay ahead there would be other celebrations. For many these celebrations would be tinged with sorrow. There were wounds and scars that would never completely heal. Loved ones that would never return. But these were not the thoughts that occupied the sleepy head of a nine year old boy.

My eyes closed, I began to drift. Outside the mood had changed; now the singing was softer and seemed to come from a great distance away . . . .

> *'There'll be bluebirds over the white cliffs of Dover,*
> *Tomorrow, just you wait and see . . .'*

Twenty

Celebrations

WHEN WORD SPREAD that our greengrocer had a shipment of oranges, or rarer still bananas, then a queue would quickly form, lengthening until it had almost reached the end of the street. On more than one occasion Mother would reach the front of the queue only to be told:

'Sorry, luv, all gone! All sold out. You'll have to wait until our next delivery.'

Once mother overheard a lady say that she would sell her soul for some oranges, or it may have been bananas! It really upset Mum, she had taken the remark very seriously and felt she must say something.

'You shouldn't say that, dear,' Mother gently reprimanded. 'It's such an awful thing to say.'

But despite continued shortages and on-going rationing we rejoiced that the war, for us, was finally over, at least in Europe. Slowly the reality began to sink in. No more bombs, no more blackout; and the wail of the sirens replaced by the joyful peal of church bells. In the months and years to come there would be much to do: bomb sites still to be cleared, buildings restored and rebuilt and people to be re-housed; but now it was a time for celebration.

Every street and road had its own display of flags and bunting. Many streets were left with blackened circles scorched into them by VE day bonfires, and more bonfires were planned. In the days ahead there would be parades, displays, illuminations and dancing.

Late one evening Mum and Dad took me to the seafront to see the victory trolley-bus. It was getting dark when we arrived and already a crowd had gathered.

'Here it comes!' shouted someone, and moments later it came into view ablaze with coloured lights on its front, its back and its sides. Lights even extended along its two slender arms. We cheered and shouted as it slowly and almost silently passed beside us and continued on its illuminated tour of the Portsmouth streets.

Then there was the tank parade. Earlier Mum and I had caught the bus to North End to join the crowds standing by the roadside. People crammed the narrow pavements straining to catch a glimpse of the huge army tanks as they slowly trundled past us, their caterpillar treads squealing and grinding, making the ground around us vibrate and shake. I stood there opened-mouthed, breathing in the fumes and adding my own voice to the incredible noise as we waved, cheered and shouted our thanks to the brave soldiers seated on their tanks smiling and waving back at us.

In our own Milton Park special events were being laid on for us children. In the evenings I would run to the park to meet up with my other school friends and watch the free nightly entertainments.

'What's on tonight?'

'Puppets!'

Or it might have been Punch and Judy, or Jugglers, or a Magician, perhaps a Ventriloquist.

We would all gather round as each act was performed against a background of leafy trees and then go on to play our own games afterwards. On the very last night people of all ages gathered around the bandstand to listen to a dance band. Even my Mum and Dad were there! We heard the unmistakable music of Glen Miller and other popular wartime songs sounding out across the park while more and more couples joined in dancing around the bandstand perimeter.

As the music continued I joined some of my school friends and we began to run and play behind the standing onlookers. And then as the evening drew to a close, and the sky darkened, a girl that I had sometimes seen at school asked me if I would like to dance with her. I hesitated.

'Can you dance?' she asked me.

I shook my head. 'No.' I said.

But she didn't seem to hear and the next moment she had taken my hand in hers and I found myself being swept on to the dance area.

I was not quite sure what my right leg or left leg were supposed to be doing, but it didn't seem to matter for she seemed quite happy.

'See, you can dance.' she smiled. Suddenly I was moving to the music and I didn't want it to stop. I wanted it to go on forever!

But all too soon it had ended and I watched as my partner disappeared into the crowd and only then did I join my mother and father as together we made our mass exit from the park.

August 15th 1945 VJ day

'Now it really is all over!'

The Prime Minister, Clement Attlee, broadcasting to the nation said: "The last of our enemies is laid low."

The King also spoke: "Our hearts are full to

overflowing, as are your own . . ."

We rejoiced and gave thanks as we heard the news that Japan had surrendered.[27] Once again there were more celebrations, dancing, singing, illuminations and exploding fireworks! Flags flew, and bonfires blazed.

Later we would learn more of the terrible effects of the Hiroshima and Nagasaki bombing, and the nuclear threat that now shadowed our world.

---

[27] The official surrender and signing under General Koiso Kuniaki did not take place until September 2nd.

Twenty-one

Afterwards

My first visit to the Cinema

THE LIGHTS DIMMED and the curtains slowly opened. I was about to see my very first Hollywood movie in a real cinema.

Earlier Mrs Wiggins, our next door neighbour, had kindly invited me, along with her grandson Carroll and two of his friends, to the Gaiety[28] cinema.

'We're just off to the pictures,' she said. 'Would you like to come with us?'

Would I like to come!

'It's quite suitable,' she continued turning to my Mother. 'It's a Walt Disney film *–Bambi.'*

On our arrival at the cinema an official looking man resplendent in uniform had greeted us at the

---

[28] Later to become a Supermarket. as were other cinemas in the city.

doors, and after climbing the carpeted steps up to the circle, a waiting usherette directed us by torchlight to our seats.

As the film commenced Mrs Wiggins leaned over and whispered in my ear.

'This is only the supporting film,' she informed me, 'Just a cheap film,' she added dismissively, 'before the big picture starts.'

The film was a western. It may have been only a second feature but I watched awestruck as Johnny Mac Brown, on horseback, thundered across the screen. After a terrific gun fight, fought with limitless ammunition, he had finally brought the "bad men" to justice, leaving us cheering as he rode off into the sunset and the credits.

Of course, I enjoyed the Technicolored Bambi that followed but, for me, it was Johnny Mac Brown who had won the day and was now my hero!

The Circus

Sea mist covered the Southsea common almost obscuring the sunlight. It was early morning. As Mother and I walked across the damp grass we could hear the muffled sounds of hammers striking metal. *The Circus was in town!*

Already the two giant "King Poles" were in position and a scattering of caravans and trailers encircled them. We made our way to one of the caravans, Mother hesitated and then tapped on the door which eventually opened and a circus lady stared down at us.

'I'm afraid you're too early, dear,' she said in answer to Mother's question. 'The booking office doesn't open until eleven. Didn't you see the poster?'

We had seen the poster. I had read it and re-read it. In bold, colourful letters it announced: *"Sir Robert Fossett's Gigantic Circus coming to Portsmouth."* I had stared at it for ages and knew almost every word by heart except the part about the booking office!

'You'll have to come back later.' continued the lady.

'But I've come all the way from Milton,' Mother replied. 'I'm not sure that I can.'

I must have looked utterly crestfallen and the woman noticing my distress suddenly seemed to have a change of heart.

'Wait here.' she said and disappearing into the caravan reappeared minutes later with two precious tickets!

Later that evening I found myself seated on a wooden bench next to my brother looking down at the sawdust covered ring. I was about to see my very first circus. I could hardly wait for the show to begin.

Eventually the lights brightened, the music began to play and the Ringmaster, cracking his whip, stepped into the ring. I was about to experience, for myself, the sights, sounds and smells that make up a circus. It was what I had so long dreamed about.

I watched the beautifully groomed horses with their flying manes as they cantered around the ring, snorting and tossing their heads. I fell in love with the pretty girl who rode bareback on a white horse, and I held my breath as the daring trapeze artists somersaulted under the very roof of the big top. It was just as my Dad had said it would be. And, of course, there were all the clowns. How we laughed at their antics! It was, I remembered, a clown waving to me from his caravan, all those years ago, that had first fuelled my love for the circus.

After it was all over, Bert and I walked through the ring, now thronged with people, and out into the menagerie where we could take a closer look at the animals.

'Well, what did you think of it all?' Bert asked. 'Did you enjoy it?'

One look at my flushed face was all the answer my brother needed. As we walked homeward across the darkened common I had already made up my mind that I would have my own circus. Even if it were only a table-top one! I would save up my pocket money and buy lead animals which were only now, after the war, just coming back into the shops. I would call it:

"Jupp's Gigantic Circus!"

The football match

It was Saturday afternoon and I was about to see my first football match. Together with Richard and some of my school friends I was on my way to Fratton Park home of the famous Pompey football club.

As we neared the stadium our pace quickened and we merged with the crowds of people, coming from all directions, each making their way to one of the many entrances. I followed Richard and the others through one of the gates, where we paid our money[29] and clicked ourselves through the heavy turnstiles.

'Come on,' said Richard. 'Quick, let's get behind the goal!'

We ran and dodged our way down the terraces and just managed to find a place by the wall where we could stand close to the goal.

'You'll get a good view of the action, here!' shouted one of my friends.

The sunlit pitch was a vivid green, so bright you could almost see each blade of grass while the white goal posts, the painted perimeter lines and other areas, stood out in sharp contrast. *The previous time I had been to Fratton Park, was that night when I had watched the combined services display with Brenda in those early days of the war. It all seemed a long time ago.*

---

[29] Nine pence old money for a First Team Match and six-pence for a Reserve Team Match.

The terraces and stands were now almost full; all eyes were focused on the players' tunnel. Suddenly a cheer went up as the visiting team ran on to the pitch for their warm-up. It was followed by a tumultuous roar as Pompey in their royal blue shirts and white shorts took to the pitch amid strains of *"Play up Pompey!"* reverberating around the ground.

"Play up, Pompey,
Pompey play up!
Play up, Pompey,
Pompey play up!"

I stood there, open mouthed, swept along with the crowd. Everything seemed larger than life, the pace was terrific, the leather ball swerved and sped across the grass, often going past the goals and into the crowd. Sometimes beating the goalie and finding the back of the goal-net. A deafening roar would immediately follow with the fans shouting and jumping on the terraces, and those in the stands getting to their feet and applauding.

It was all so different from the street football I was used to, or even the football we played in the park. For the first time I learnt about *throw-ins, free-kicks and off-sides.* I'm not sure I understood about off-sides, but then, according to the Pompey crowd, neither did the referee!

I loved every minute of it, and after the final whistle I couldn't wait to get to the park where, with my friends, we could play out our own match; we would be the stars, watched and applauded by thousands of unseen, imaginary spectators.

Holiday

It was the evening when our coach finally reached its destination: the pretty little Sussex town of Shoreham-by-Sea. Dad, mother, and I stepped outside to be immediately greeted by Brenda and her mother.

'How lovely to see you all!' said Mrs Webber, embracing my Mother.

For the next few days we would be staying at her cottage in old Shoreham, but first it was decided we would make a small detour across the footbridge that spanned the harbour and on to the beach.

Brenda and I went ahead leaving our parents to do some "catching up." At first I felt a little awkward, I think Brenda probably felt the same. Although there was only a year or so difference in our ages she was now much taller and seemed quite grown up, she was certainly more knowledgeable. Later she told me that she knew how babies were made!

'How are babies made?' I asked her.

'You're too young to know,' she said. And that was that.

As we crunched our way across the shingle and stood at the water's edge, Brenda bent down and picked up a pebble.

'Can you play *ducks and drakes?*' she asked. And before I could reply she had sent her pebble skimming across the waves where it bounced once, twice, three times even four, before it finally sank out of sight.

'I can sometimes make it skim six or even seven times,' she said.

The challenge was now on. My first attempt hit a wave with a giant plop and disappeared beneath the surface.

'You need a flat stone,' Brenda told me.

However hard I tried, and much to my annoyance, there seemed no way I could beat her. But any reserve or shyness there may have been between us had now quickly evaporated and, before we made our way back to the cottage, it was as though we had never been separated.

Over the next week we played together, explored Shoreham, and caught the bus to nearby Brighton. We visited its famous aquarium and waxworks where Brenda insisted on taking me to the *Chamber of Horrors* which wasn't the least bit scary. Strangely enough during our whole time together I don't think we ever mentioned the war.

All too soon our brief holiday came to an end and once more we were back on the coach waving goodbye, but promising we would see each other again.

For a long time I sat very quietly, deep in thought, staring through the coach window with Shoreham swiftly disappearing from view and Sussex giving way to a familiar Hampshire.

What lay ahead?

Another new school to go to, making new friends, certainly many new experiences. For most of my childhood I had only known war. There had been times when I had experienced fear even terror, and yet it had not been an unhappy childhood, in many ways just an ordinary childhood but in an extraordinary time.

Together, as a family, living in a strategic, often targeted city, we had escaped injury, separation and loss. We had found a shelter from a terrible storm. The clouds had been driven away; as a Nation we had been blessed.

As I continued my journey into peacetime I hoped it would remain that way for a very long time to come.

Postscript

Many years later, together with my wife and two of my young children, I decided to take a nostalgic trip back to Reigate.

Our first stop was Redhill Common. Once again I clambered up those steep tree clad slopes, as I had long ago with my cousin Audrey, only this time it was with my two children, each of us slipping, sliding, and clinging tenaciously to the great protruding tree roots. A short stay and then on to the bustling Reigate High Street, with the little Town Hall seemingly unchanged and my favourite toy shop opposite, *La Trobes,* that I had visited with Renie, still there.

Our journey now took us towards Doods Road, first stopping at Wray Common with its ancient brick windmill, still standing tall and proud, and then on to my old house which I approached with a mixture of memories and emotions. Would it, I wondered, still be as I remembered? Would it be recognisable?

With a little apprehension I knocked on the front door and after some initial hesitation the lady occupant kindly allowed us inside.

To my surprise little seemed to have altered. It looked smaller but I had expected that and, of course, the furniture had changed. My Dad's treasured piano no longer occupied its space in the front room, and the table that had dominated both living rooms in Doods Road and Warren Avenue no longer there. But the hallway and the narrow stairs were as I remembered them.

It was nineteen thirty-nine once more. I was back standing on the little landing, with that first eerie wailing siren still ringing in my ears, while I waited, rooted to the spot, for my Mother to return from the street below.

It was now time to move into the garden. Again there had been few alterations. It was still long and narrow and the high hedge where Hilda's head would suddenly appear was still there but, with a shock, I realized that I could now see over it and into the adjoining gardens.

We continued down the path until we came to the spot where my 'crocodile pond' would have stood. The old galvanised bath was nowhere to be seen, but my children knew all about it. Later it would play a part in their bedtime stories.

We were coming to the far end of the garden and I

couldn't wait to show them that special place where the iron railings had stood; the same ones I had so often pressed my face against, watching and waving, as those wonderful locomotives steamed their way past my garden.

But this was to be my greatest disappointment. There were no railings. Sadly they had been replaced by an ugly brick wall. The railway lines and the trains that travelled on them were no longer visible.

With memories reignited I took a last lingering look. It was time for us to leave. We said our good-byes and began our journey back to Portsmouth — *home*.